# The TAO of Dishwashing

## Tasking a master soul

Raja

Published by I AM Unlimited Publishing
Atlanta, Georgia 30311
e-mail info@iamunlimited.org
Cover Illustration and Design by Rob Jerome Jones - Bright Raven Graphics Atlanta, Georgia
e.mail brightraven@bellsouth.com

Copyright 2018 by S.L. "Raja" Crumby
Library of Congress Catalog Card Number 2013915360

Revised from The Tao of Dishwashing - Preparing Your Soul for the New Millennium

First Edition, First Printing September 1999

Note: The GYE NYAME (jeh N-yah-mee) symbol used on the cover and at the chapter headings, is a Ghanaian symbol which represents the belief in the supremacy of God in the Ghanaian society. Its literal interpretation is: "EXCEPT GOD" or 'TIS ONLY GOD," and reflects God's power over all creation.
Source: The Adinkra Dictionary, Bruce W. Willis, 1998 Pyramid Complex, Washington, DC

All rights reserved. No part of this book may be reproduced, stored in retrieval systems or transmitted in any form or by any means without the written consent of the publisher.
ISBN: 978-1-929526-04-8

# Contents

Acknowledgments and Dedication ........................................................ 5
Introduction .................................................................................... 7

Chapter 1:
    Where We are Versus Where We are Headed:
    Charting a Course for the New Millennium ...................... 13

        The Re-ordering of Cosmic Energy ......................... 15
        Beings of Destiny ....................................................... 17
        The Journey Home .................................................... 21
        The Crops of "Hybrid Seed" ..................................... 24
        Why the Children? ..................................................... 26
        The Myth of "Private Gardens" .............................. 28
        A Precursor to Every War ......................................... 30
        Fruit After It's Own Kind ......................................... 32
        The Crops of Hybrid Seeds continued ................... 33
        Toward Conscious Change ....................................... 34
        Rising to the Occasion ............................................. 39
        Recovering Your Genius ........................................... 42
        Summary ..................................................................... 46

Chapter 2:
    Who Am I? - The Dilemma of Personal Identification ... 49

        Through the Eyes of a Child ................................... 51
        Social Consciousness Checklist ............................... 53
        Summary ..................................................................... 54

Chapter 3:
    Showing Up in Pursuit of the Kingdom ............................ 55

        The Role of the "Nurses" ......................................... 55
        The "Non-Generic" Kingdom of God .................... 60
        Summary ..................................................................... 62

Chapter 4:
    Being in Integrity .................................................................. 65

        Following the Law of Your Soul ............................. 69
        Summary ..................................................................... 71

**Chapter 5:**

Motivation ................................................................................ 73

        Life's Four Basic Motivators ............................................ 74
        A Willingness to Buck Tradition .................................... 79
        Summary .......................................................................... 81

**Chapter 6:**

    The Anatomy of "A-TASK" ............................................... 85

        Passion Deferred ............................................................. 87
        A-TASK" Defined ........................................................... 88
        Summary .......................................................................... 90

**Chapter 7:**

    The Analogy of Dishwashing ............................................. 93

        Summary .......................................................................... 95

**Chapter 8:**

    Assessing the Washing Environment:
    Your Spiritual Practice ...................................................... 97

        Toward True Worship ..................................................... 99
        Summary ........................................................................ 101

**Chapter 9:**

    Scraping Your Plate: Getting Rid of the Baggage ........... 103

        The Battleground of Interpersonal Relationship . 104
        Summary ........................................................................ 108

**Chapter 10:**

    Pre-Rinsing: The Process of Introspection and
    Self-Observation ............................................................... 111

        Your "Achilles Heel" ..................................................... 112
        Creating a "Collective Achilles Heel" ......................... 116
        Summary ........................................................................ 119

Chapter 11:
> Preparing the Water: Engaging the Spirit ......... 121
>> Monitoring Your "Self-Talk" ......... 123
>> The Two Most Powerful Words ......... 123
>> An Attitude of Gratitude ......... 125
>> Moving Your Body ......... 126
>> Sitting Still ......... 128
>> Reading for Value ......... 129
>> Summary ......... 131

Chapter 12:
> Putting Your Dishes in the Water:
> The Process of Surrender ......... 135
>> Cast Your Bread Upon the Waters ......... 137
>> Summary ......... 141

Chapter 13:
> Soaking Your Dishes: The Process of Meditation ......... 143
>> Uprooting Deeply-seated Deposits
>> of Mis-Identity ......... 146
>> Summary ......... 149

Chapter 14:
> Washing Your Dishes:
> The Practical Application of Principle ......... 151
>> Know Your Patterns ......... 151
>> At Whit's End ......... 155
>> A Cry in the Wilderness ......... 156
>> Back on Track ......... 157
>> Summary ......... 159

Chapter 15:
> Rinsing Your Dishes: The Final Clearing ......... 161
>> A Walking Meditation ......... 162
>> Summary ......... 163

Chapter 16:

    Drying Your Dishes: The Process of Reflection .......... 165

        Returning Home ...................................................... 166
        Summary .................................................................. 169

Chapter 17:

    Staying Connected ........................................................ 171

        Indifference versus Detachment ........................... 171
        A Willingness to Persevere .................................... 175
        Summary .................................................................. 177

Chapter 18:

    Where is Your Talent? ................................................... 179

        Your Soul - The Ultimate Dish ............................. 179
        The Little Foxes that Destroy the Vine ............... 180
        The Parable of the Talents .................................... 182
        Polo Horses .............................................................. 183
        A Self-Test ............................................................... 184
        Wonderful News ..................................................... 186
        Making the Leap .................................................... 187

    They Said You Were Not Ready - A Poem by Raja ........ 191

    Author's Contact and Other Works ................................ 193

# Acknowledgments and Dedication

## *Washing My First Set of Dishes*

There are many persons to whom I owe great tribute for the life processes that have become this book. My life has been abundantly sprinkled with those who have, quite often, inadvertently yet effectively tutored me along the way. Chief among these are my Mother, Nellie Elizabeth Ingol, my Father, Samuel Herr Crumby and my stepfather, James Ingol. I dedicate this book to you. The estrangement I experienced from you at an early age has me hard-pressed to recall any significantly nurturing father/son or mother/son interactions. An exchange of a simple "I love you" was never a part of the culture we developed. Yet, in looking at my life, in terms of inner strengths and gifts, I am clear that the two of you were the perfect sponsors for my soul, and are the greatest gifts I have ever received. I am also clear that you both love me.

Dad, there were times, growing up, when your not being there was a source of great pain for me. Yet, as I've come to a fuller understanding of life's processes, I'm truly grateful for your example of one of the greatest lessons of my life - how to let go and move on when it is clear that an experience has run its course. Though I didn't see it then, my ability to unfold into a strong, self-determinate individual is largely due to being "left to my own devices" which afforded me time and opportunity to discover my own resources. I could have embarked my life feeling bitter and quite the victim, with, seemingly, no choice but to hold you responsible for the potential undoing of my life. Yet, having traveled a wonderful circle of growth and unfoldment, here we stand, in many ways, as "carbon copies" and friends.

Mom, when I left home at age seventeen, I felt, at the same time, wounded and free. Those were difficult days. I spent many nights lying in bed at the YMCA in Akron, Ohio, crying my eyes out. The events that transpired between us left me tattered and torn. I'm sure they had a great impact upon you, also. In fact, I suspect they still do. I would like for you to know that our impasse was born of a particularly needful and powerful point of soul to soul interaction. And though deeply painful, it set me forth upon the path to releasing the energy that sponsors this book, my music and all that I do. That is the energy of self-love.

This acknowledgment would not be complete without honoring the input of my stepfather, James Ingol. Living under his roof for fifteen years demanded that I take on and bear the weight of a relentless assault on my worth. Having been told that I was not and never would be at home, as well as that, like my father, I would never be anything was hurtful and off-putting. Yet, those assaults brought me face-to-face with the primal tenet of my life purpose - to model an unassailable sense of self-love as a precursor to teaching others how to accept love.

Few were the days when peace prevailed between us. Consequently, I struggled mightily to garner a sense of comfort and belonging. Any one of several intense encounters that ensued could have easily broken my spirit or, at least, left me bitter or rendered my heart cold. But that is not the path I chose. As I was reminded recently by my brother, your namesake, James, I stood strong, even refusing to cry as you laid into me with a belt, switch, broom stick, extension chord, or whatever was at hand. Though clearly a back-door method that deliberately shunned the "high road," this wonderful test for my soul never divested me of the inherent respect for you as my parent, or of the strength that was gifted to my soul.

Without the cleverly disguised input from each of you, my impact upon others would not be as heart-felt, and my life would not be as rewarding. As a result, I live my life and do my work while reveling in the great pleasure of having become anchored, early on, in the truth of myself as a Master Soul. I honor the role that you all played in sponsoring me into the world, rearing me and sending me forth with God Speed. Whether you know it or not, you have each been and remain great lights in my world. My hope is that you have come to afford yoursekf the grace to look beyond your perceived faults and failures to see this great truth. This book is my testament that I am free from my past. And with my love and appreciation, may you each be free to enjoy each moment of your existene; delighting in the truth that you played your roles well. I love each of you.

*Introduction*

A life-long quest for self-knowledge and a true sense of purpose has led me to accept that my response to each of life's opportunities determines my destiny or the way my life ultimately unfolds. I believe that each thought we think, each feeling we harbor, every word we speak, and the motivation behind each of our actions serve to mold our character, which builds and maintains the only reputation that ultimately matters: our reputation with "Self."

As a child, I often spent time sitting alone in the woods pondering such questions as: "Who am I?" - "Why am I here?" - "Why am I in this situation?"- "When will it get better?" and "What will I ultimately do in life?" My initial inquiry was projected toward God, who was "somewhere out there." Ultimately, as I grew older and wiser - realizing that no external, overriding intervention was in store - I began to accept more responsibility for my life's direction. It was then that I began to speak to and listen from my heart - to the God who lives within.

When I've listened to my heart, I've always gotten answers, even when I didn't clearly see or understand them or like what I was shown. Quite often, the directive was to perfect or eliminate an aspect of my life that no longer served me, and to which I was no longer committed to being in alignment. The challenge was that, due to my limited perception of my personal power, I had gotten stuck, and seemed neither ready, willing nor able to let go and move on to my next highest good.

So it is with each of us. When the passionate fires of connectedness cease to burn between us and our relationships with people, places and things, we have choices and decisions to make. Our personal history documents that how we respond in these crucial moments has a long-term effect on our sense of self-worth; for these choices will either induce or thwart important and timely opportunities for growth.

I, like most, had looked outside myself to relationships, work, educational opportunities, and religious/social connections to quench the fire and yearning for a lasting sense of inner fulfillment. I was determined to "make my mark" and, thereby, quell the voices of the ghosts of inadequacy and failure that plagued my youth. After experiencing many of what I called "near misses," I arrived at the realization that my belief system or consciousness about what success means holds the key to my ability or inability to master and enjoy my life. With this revelation as my guide, I was determined to discover my integral, internal truth. So I decided to return home - to the center of my being - to sit, again, with that little boy with the penchant for asking big questions.

In making the journey within, I discovered a principle aspect of my life purpose. It is something that is as natural and right as rain...something that I consciously and joyously embrace. It is my commitment to employ every ounce of my being to help you understand how your life experiences are geared to aid your quest to live your true identity. It is to aid you in really knowing and loving yourself, as I have learned to do. This is my gift and my genius. I also feel that knowing, accepting and loving yourself is the surest way to get you to see others more clearly, and to establish mutually rewarding relationships with them, as well.

I've found that my work can be done in simple ways, such as allowing you to merge into traffic while I hold a space for you. I will open a door for you or help you pick up something you may have dropped. I do so in other subtle ways, such as smiling when I consistently think good thoughts of you, though you may not know that I know who you are. I choose to re-present love, and extend this energy into your heart, so that you will feel uplifted in times when life seems overwhelming, and soar when you know that all of life is full of wonder.

As I embrace you through sharing the insights and inspirations of this and other books, my "The Art of Living" music project and other audio presentations, I will remind you of your Soul's urge to purge itself of any tendency toward fear, mediocrity and limitation. I will encourage you to connect, unfold and to experience all...to contribute to the enhancement of human life, I will admonish you to be excellent and free.

It has taken a while (many lifetimes within this one life experience, many endings and new beginnings) to assimilate what is shared in this book. I write for the simple reason that, in my quest for wholeness and inner fulfillment, I have discovered the principle importance of listening to my spirit...of honoring the needs of my soul. My soul says "Write the book, share your insights." In its quest for the ultimate integrity or "Godhood," the Soul - which is the vessel or "dish" into which is gathered the sum total of all we think, feel, speak, believe, and act upon - is eternally engaged in assimilating life experience. Forever gathering, assessing and recording the energy we release, it is as engaged during the seeming insignificant moments of our lives as it is during those moments to which we grant the most significance. So, in reality, every moment we live and breathe is a "defining moment."

The title, The Tao of Dishwashing, came to me at the urging of my Soul. It just sort of "popped in on me" like one's supervisor might do while delivering a new work order. Tao (pronounced Dow) is a Chinese word which basically means "the way"- the simplistic way. The choice of this word has no significance for my religious beliefs, nor is this book the dishwasher/busboy's guide to career advancement - at least not exclusively. As an offering from the platter of my collective experience, its content is based upon my belief that each of us has what it takes (within) to create that which brings joy, peace and fulfillment to our lives, while simultaneously contributing to the uplifting of humanity - if but one person at a time. It is rooted in my belief that we are all here by choice, and inhabit circumstances that promote the growth of our humanity. Dishwashing is my metaphor for clearing the path that leads to understanding and living from our Soul's intent, purpose, kingdom, and domain.

In order to unfold into Mastery, our soul requires that we become emotionally enrolled, invigorated and truly "present" with It in each of Its undertakings - great and small. Only then can the deliberate steps from mediocrity to Mastery be taken. Only then will we engage the path that will reveal our true Genius. Toward this end, I believe each person, event and circumstance entering our life comes bearing a gift. Rarely do we see through the illusion to the core to know the true nature of that gift or its exact location within the experience. Though each is different - some are pearls, some silver, others gold, some sticks, others stones - all are of great importance to the building of our souls. All are priceless and authentically empowering, regardless of how mundane, insignificant or even threatening they appear.

Through honoring everyone and everything entering our lives with our presence (or attention, respect and highest intent) our souls begin to flourish, opening us to receiving that which our hearts desire most: a glimpse at Godhood - our true legacy. It is in this space of alignment with my soul's desire that the urge to bring forth this book was born. It is in this space that the "Fruits of the Spirit" - those elements which constitute your Personal Mastery - will be revealed.

In pondering the unlimited potential of a new millennium, I set forth (in chapter one) that we are in the midst of tumultuous change as well as spiritually fortuitous times. Our desire to experience ourselves in our Divinity is seeking its rightful expression. In order to institute conscious change, it is necessary to come to terms with where we are and how we arrived here. It is my desire to aid you in making the leap in consciousness that will afford you the drive needed to make the connection. My intent is that this book instigates a personal and interactive journey. Toward this end, I have included exercises and affirmations to aid you in working through its principles. These exercises provide a space for peering within, so that you will, hopefully come to know and embrace yourself at deeper levels.

Will implementing these ideas and principles make me rich? - you ask. While material prosperity is not its focus, this book lays the foundation for prosperity to unfold on all levels - even as your soul prospers. In order to allow prosperity to flow, you must release your excuses for being mediocre and your attachment to the idea that someone or something can hold you down against your will. If you are willing to allow your Soul's "divine agenda" to fuel your life, it will propel you beyond the illusion that racism, sexism, poverty, or someone else's assessment of your potential has any real power to determine your destiny.

You and I are connected. We have traveled this path before, and I look forward to meeting you again. It is my desire that we stand together on the shores of a greater understanding and, together, wade in the sea of human commonality. Consequently, I have a personal interest in the growth of your humanity. So do the work. Make it personal. Delve into the innermost parts of your Being to take a clear look at what you've created to date. Be honest with yourself about your motivations in life, and be willing to own complete responsibility for the course your life has taken and takes from this point forward. Should you embark the journey, you will amass the power to reclaim complete ownership of your soul.

As one humanity, we have the opportunity to ride the crest of a universal wave of heightened spiritual awareness. We arrived on this plane committed and equipped to do so. This is the time to make the journey. Quite often, a bit of "tweaking" is all that is required. At other times, we may need a major overhaul. There are also those times when embarking the path that leads to the fulfillment of our deepest desires may require a new engine or even a completely new vehicle. You will know the steps that are needed for your journey.

One thing is for certain, there is a feast being made ready. On the table are the fulfillment of life purpose and the unfolding of Individual Genius. The host (universal source and supply) is extending you an invitation. How you show up at the door is not important. Whether, Black, Yellow, Red, White, Mixed; rich or poor; youthful or more mature; presumably bound or free, your potential for Genius and the path to wholeness are resident within you. They can be summoned, through self-mastery, whatever your race, age, occupation, physical, financial, or other conditions. What is most important is whether your desire to feast at the finest of life's banquet tables (as the guest of honor who ultimately owns the restaurant) is great enough to begin with The Tao of Dishwashing.

- Raja

# Chapter 1

*Where We Are Versus Where We Are Headed:*

*Charting a Course for the New Millennium*

*"In a world that seems to be falling apart because we're so far apart, we've got to come together, and find a better way."*

Anytime We Come Together - A "World Anthem " - Raja

My desire to be an instrument for human awakening has endowed me with a certain receptivity to the pulse of mass consciousness. As I travel to speak and share the message of my music, I sense an undercurrent of dissatisfaction, non-fulfillment and dismay resonating from the souls of many. Yet, this is not a "bad thing"- the stuff of foreboding and dread. This "divine discontent," if you will, is evidence of the early stages of response to a calling that rests upon our collective lives. It speaks to a relentless hope and insatiable quest for self-understanding and a peaceful existence. Many are responding by: dialing psychic hot-lines; studying books and tapes on self-improvement; and attending religious services, seminars, workshops, ashrams, life enhancement expos, and psychic fairs in record numbers. Others attempt to expand their conscious awareness and/or quell their fears through the use of drugs, alcohol, sex, and other stimulants.

There are also those who respond by purchasing guns, mace and sophisticated security systems, and by stockpiling supplies before "heading for the hills." Yet, resting beneath the pursuits of psychological/material/sensual gratification and personal security lies a deeper sense within our souls. Collectively, we are being called upon to gaze into the mirror of cosmic reflection, to contemplate how we might begin to shape the next thousand years.

There is a sense that we are at the most pivotal time of our lives. Standing within the counsel of our innermost thoughts and feelings, we are clear that, historically, our attention has not been given to building a world that mirrors our highest senses of humanitarianism and benevolence. We have, instead, focused the majority of our efforts on smaller, self-centered agenda. We have chosen to square off beneath the banners of nationalism, religion, politics, ethnicity, racism, and sexism - the favorite bastions of our altered-ego selves. Consequently, in direct proportion to our wildest imaginings, we have grown increasingly disconnected from and fearful of each other.

Transfixed by the events that unfold in our world, our inclination is no longer toward a belief in the inherent good in our fellow human beings. Our default consciousness favors seeing ourselves as vulnerable and in need of tools for defending ourselves against ever-encroaching enemies to our survival. Yet, a major challenge has arisen. Simply stated, we are having great difficulty identifying this enemy or anticipating his or her actions. The fact that most of us do not know the neighbor two doors down on either side denotes a grave lack of community and trust. It bespeaks a quiet fear that a potential monster may live beside us. This distrust is reflective of a void where inner security and connectedness are concerned. Overshadowed by fear, we've abandoned the idea that there is a vital, universal presence that preserves our immortality.

With gun violence on the rise, we are quick to point to our constitutional right to bear arms as the source of our zeal for gun toting. Yet, at our core, it is the offensive energies of hatred and fear that cause us to so eloquently rise up to defend our need to defend. It is these energies that draw to us those anticipated events that we must, ultimately, defend ourselves against. By failing to grasp a fundamental understanding of the power of our thoughts, fears, anxieties, and expectations, we have inherited an inner sense of powerlessness that is reflected in the way we have structured our world.

Our minds are hard-pressed to imagine a time, place or world where there would be no need for weapons to defend our false senses of territory. Yet, the potential for such a world exists. Yes its seeds struggle to ward-off the life-thwarting assaults waged by the abortive pesticides of hatred and fear. But its tender sprouts have taken certain if but furtive root within the garden of collective consciousness.

It is a fact that every thought we think has the potential of our most heartfelt prayer. The more emotional the thought, the more magnetic and attractive it becomes to the creative forces charged with bringing it to fruition. In other words, the more we allow our emotions to embrace and nurture an idea, the more power we give that idea to establish our reality and chart our course. How often have we heard stories of someone fleeing one city in favor of another in an attempt to escape the threat of violence only to have violence come upon them in their newly chosen place of "safe-haven." This is the "Law of Attraction" at work within our thought and feeling natures.

An understanding of the workings of this Universal Principle is a prerequisite for creating conscious change in our lives. It will also provide proof-positive that - at the deepest levels of our being, beyond our conscious awareness and intent - we choose and create every experience that we have. This is a leap in consciousness that many souls continue to resist; for to embrace this truth would put our old friends the "devil" and "random fate" out of business. Concerning fear, the message of this law is quite clear: Taking precautionary measures is a sign of wisdom. Yet, the choice to embrace fear as a healthy motivation for life change will result in your being stalked by fear until you conquer it or it overtakes you.

There are those who feel that a certain degree of fear is a healthy life additive. I think not, and choose to embrace the biblical wisdom of II Timothy 1:7 which says: "For God has not given us the spirit of fear; but of power and of love and of a sound mind." The key to getting beyond what is termed by some as: "False Evidence Appearing Real," is in finding its source within our consciousness and uprooting it. Examining our beliefs about our vulnerability and replacing them with the self-empowering reality of our eternal nature will expose the futility of fear. We will then become empowered to master our emotional nature, which is the key to mastering our life.

## A "Reordering" of Cosmic Energy

In spite of our penchant for fear, THIS IS OUR TIME! It is an auspicious time of expansion and unfoldment; for we have the wonderful opportunity to have our self-imposed fears and limitations lifted, if we choose to have it so. As a response to our undying quest for a fuller understanding of our role in the cosmic play of things, we are beginning to embrace the fact that each of us has a vested interest in contributing to the wellness of our planetary home as well as humanity at large. We chose to be here at this time to seize an opportunity to embrace our unlimited nature. We have enrolled to play a conscious role in shifting the energy of this planet into a more harmonious octave of resonance. Held captive by the coma inducing hypnosis of societal indoctrination, many choose to slumber and sleep while the shift is occurring. Others - though they have clearly heard the call - are not fully given to the task of living consciously. Even so, a general "inner alarm" has sounded and, as a result, humanity in greater numbers is beginning to toss and turn, as we struggle to awaken from the dream.

Having had the experience of glimpsing the dream within the dream, we sense the overshadowing of an intruder in our midst. This "presence" resists all attempts toward ignorance. As an occasional night visitor that invades our comfort zones, disturbs our nests and ruffles our feathers, it seems at once familiar and unknown. Its subtle yet incessant whispers of "wake up dreamer" are sufficient to insure that there will be no rest until its presence is fully acknowledged and its intent made clear. Who is it that has made itself at home within our private thought and feeling worlds? It is the voice of our subconscious awareness calling us to emerge from our slumber to greet and embrace the truth of our Being.

Throughout society, the impetuous sound of external alarm clocks can be heard within our waking worlds. As we watch and listen to the goings-on in our global environment, we see and hear of shifts occurring at every level. Though the examples are numerous and varied such as: the fall of Communism in the Soviet Union and the dismantling of the wall dividing East and West Germany; as well as public response to the polarization in our nation's capitol; our ability to discern a rapidly emerging paradigm is - at best - muted. Yet, these and other prominent local and global events are evidence of a collective yearning for freedom, democracy and self-determination. All are indications of humanity's deep-seated - though largely subconscious - desire to release an attachment to petty differences, and shift the focus to the more panoramic view of what is best for humanity at-large. All are indicative of a relentless quest for a broader understanding of our indelible connection.

At what may appear to be the "other end of the spectrum," there is an obvious increase in crimes committed against individuals because of race, sexual preference, ethnicity, and/or religious and political persuasion. And let's not overlook the ever-present reality of wars and rumors of wars. In the face of these escalations, our conditioned responses are to: build more prisons; elect more politicians who are "tough on crime;" propagate an endless war on drugs, tobacco and domestic violence; and retain more behavioral scientists. To augment our penchant for huddling beneath the wings of fear an hysteria mongers, we send more dollars to support "fire and brimstone preachers" and "right-wing politicians" with their self-righteous stands on conservatism and morality. Meanwhile, our children are killing themselves and others in numbers that hint of a pandemic.

While some see these and other events such as the devastating tornadoes, earthquakes, flooding, and the growing phenomena of the Internet and a cashless society as signs of a dreaded Apocalypse and the imminent demise of humankind, I think not. I view the overall scheme as the purging and reordering of the energy of the planet, in preparation for the emergence of a "new collective consciousness." These events are but aspects of a process for plowing through the heavily encrusted layers of social consciousness to arrive at the core of our true and common identity. They are cosmic prompts designed to urge our humanity forward.

We are witnessing the initial results of a heightened inner urge to experience the truth of ourselves and others as Beings of Light. It is through this modality - of disruption, expansion and change - that the "fallow ground of open hearts and willing minds" will be seeded within mass consciousness. It is within this soil that the seeds of "newly awakened Godhood" will be sown. Though this leg of the journey resembles a deeper descent into darkness, it is needful to say that there is a piercing light at the end of this dank, dark tunnel.

## Beings of Destiny

Where do we - as individual human beings - stand in the midst of all that is going on? Are we hapless and ineffectual bystanders with no choice but to endure, as best we can, as these discomfiting and seemingly chaotic shifts occur? Or is it that we are intended to make a conscious and deliberate contribution to the shaping of this new world? It is my belief that our choice - yours and mine - to be present at this particular time is far from happenstance. And I am certain that we are far from hapless and ineffectual. As spiritual beings destined to be here at this time, we are in the midst of a major, self- imposed "awakening and role-call." Our inability to clearly comprehend our purpose and plight has left us in deep pain. Though we are quite prolific at ascending suffering and mollifying pain, we yearn - at a deep level - to reconnect with a clear reality concerning our existence. As a result, we are being compelled to re-member our oneness, and use that indelible connection to probe beyond what appears on stage. Only then will we comprehend what is occurring behind the curtain.

Through our self-induced suffering and the playing out of each painful drama of separation, division and dissent, we are forging an opportunity to "clean the slate," so that we may write anew upon the drawing board with which we design our reality. This incessant search for the pathway to our humanity has led to many such points of reckoning. We have staged one play after another, written, read and reread all of the reviews, and pushed ourselves to the outer boundaries of human perception. Yet we still have not "gotten it." Having grown tired of our historical, reactionary behavioral patterns, we have called forth this grandest of opportunities to finally grasp that we are as much prop designers, stage hands, playwrights, producers, and directors of these dramas as we are actors and indifferent observers. We are now ready to plumb the depths of our humanity, and use its innocence and power of proactive choice to break the cycles of our painful past. Our desire is to recover the truth of our Being and to embrace and hold it near and dear, as we would a lost child who has returned to us unharmed, after many years of hoping to see him or her again.

Though we don't intellectually understand all that is transpiring, we are at a major point of intersection on this journey toward self-awareness, wholeness and Cosmic Union. We intuitively sense that breaking free from the habitual confines of fearful thinking and defensive posturing (consequences of seeing ourselves as "only human") will reawaken us to our unlimitedness. We are positioning ourselves to leap across the abyss, in pursuit of the "core truth" that lies within each of life's paradoxes. Through shared experience, empathy and grace, we are gaining balance and poise.

Noted, throughout history, are those individuals who journeyed beyond societal consciousness (beyond the veil) to engage the inner world of intuitive guidance...who followed the higher law of their souls. This is the call that rests upon our individual lives. As we move deeper into the new millennium, we are simultaneously ushering in a new spiritual era. The energy underlying this process is having an effect that is akin to "awakening the sleeping giants." In this very moment, as the final pieces of the mosaic are being laid, this awakening process is intensifying and gaining speed. Spurred by a host of events that have stirred the deep recesses of our souls, the ranks have swelled to include a larger measure of humanity.

In pursuit of connectivity and life purpose - and having arrived at the point of clearly distinguishing the illusory dream from the truth - these individuals are awakening to their divinity. An anticipation of this awakening is spoken in Romans 8:19, which states: "For the earnest expectation of the creature waiteth for the manifestation of the Sons - and I add daughters - of God." These Enlightened Beings follow a single agenda: to know the will of Spirit, as it guides them in their roles in shifting the energy of this planet. Empowered beyond any sense of fear or limitation, their greatest desire is to manifest a world created and sustained by the energies of unconditional love, joy, harmony, and peace. Refusing to be intimidated, seduced or otherwise swayed, they are clear about the source of their power, and stand firmly within its center.

In that ego no longer rules their lives, the draws of glamour, glory, glitz, and the grandiose are neutralized when it enters into their energy fields. Without partiality toward religion, race, nationality, culture, political party, or alma mater, they take no consideration for "new thought" versus "old," for the purpose of esteeming one above the other. Their understanding is that of the "One Mind," the "One Source of thought," holding within itself an unlimited quantity and quality of vibrations and possibilities.

Motivated by the belief that this is the day wherein "It is the Father's good pleasure to give us the kingdom," these emerging God-beings - "Joint Heirs in Christ Consciousness" - are answering the call to show up and possess it. Their impact is being felt, and will be felt in greater measure in every field of human endeavor. From the arts to medicine, throughout all education and technology, in politics and spirituality, these giants will emerge to lead humanity into alternative methods of "mutual life support." Intuitively sensing energy that will initiate a major shift in our collective consciousness, many have chosen to become channels of information directed to us from the Cosmic Mind. This information will stir us - as never before - to expedite ourselves to lives "outside the box." Our opportunity is to embrace this call to remember our beginning, source and heritage as the first step to recovering the light of our own Self-knowing or individual Genius.

Who are these individuals who are called to lead the charge? Are you counted among them? A deeply penetrating look beyond the facade of ego identity will reveal that, in essence, you and they are one and the same. These are they who are without condemnation. They are the meek who are destined to inherit the Earth. A revealing quality is their ability to see beyond the darkness to the inherent presence and beauty of God in all things. They are clear that the call has gone out, and the time has come to awaken, arise and do "greater things," - those things which can only be done through love.

As inhabitants of a dynamic universe that responds to the energy we put out, we have become the personal, collective and environmental recipients of pockets of energy that are due for purging and final elimination. This energy has accumulated as a result of a self-perpetuating myth that has circulated for eons. This is a myth to which we spiritual beings masquerading as humans have paid unceasing homage. Casting ourselves in the role of limited, self-serving, tyrannical wretches, we have roamed and pillaged the Earth in blind desperation, as though there were no consequences for living without forethought, and no choice but to "get while the getting is good." The result has been a loss of integrity (integration) with our true spiritual nature. Consequently, we have embraced an illusory sense of a limited self (an image upon which we have built our lives and societies) as well as fashioned our gods. Yet, all attempts to establish solid foundations upon this sinking sand have fostered a descent into the bottomless pit of insecurity, fear and distrust.

Through ignorance (or ignoring the signs), we fail to see that - within the realm of presumed disconnectedness, under the influence of self-doubt and insecurity, beneath the suppressive thumb of fear and defensiveness, there are no solid foundations; and there can never be peace. Yet, there is a bona-fide need for guns, tanks, bombs, laws governing conduct, more prisons, courses in self-defense, victims, perpetrators, affirmative action, and, yes, large doses of religion. In our current configuration, we have them all - most of them in excess.

## The Journey Home

*"Anytime We Come Together, get our egos out of the way, that's the time our souls will treasure, that's the time we'll be swept away"*

— Anytime We Come Together..A "World Anthem" - Raja

The time has come for us to journey home (within) to rediscover our true nature, and to live from its center. We have arrived at this point as the result of a yearning in our collective consciousness to rid ourselves of old thought patterns, social constructs and self-images that are no longer useful for our journey into the light. The method by which this will be obtained is one of facing all of our fears, dislikes, hatreds, and "am nots" in the Cosmic mirror of the I AM. Only then will we see ourselves and all things at their core truth. We have the choice to rise to the occasion and create new paradigms, or to simply remain asleep through attempting to recycle old patterns of behavior.

In choosing to be "altered-ego guided" by bucking the tide of change, we draw to ourselves opportunities to understand that there is a force at work that is greater than our individual, egotistical designs. There is a collective energy in motion that is drawing us to a point of self-reconciliation. An important aspect of this energy is reflected in the fact that casting judgment and disparity upon the lives, worth and actions of others is bringing a swifter recompense of reward. That reward is the opportunity to "walk in unfamiliar shoes" so that we might grasp the intricacies of our common plight.

Our evolutionary process demands that we tear down the walls of ego-illusion and self-deceit - the primary caretakers of our sense of separation. To facilitate the process, our lives are being bombarded with challenges that - if seen clearly and embraced for their gift - would empower us to both rediscover ourselves at our spiritual core and embrace our inter-connectedness. These highly discomfiting experiences are synonymous with being made to wear shoes that we feel neither fit our feet nor style. Their object is to bring us into alignment with this fundamental measure of Universal Truth: "in that God is all, we are one." Therefore, as we judge others, we judge God and ourselves.

As we grope for "cosmic understanding," the release of this static energy is creating varying responses within our inner and outer worlds. From unsettling ripples to earth-shattering explosions, events that many consider horrific, terrible and wicked continue to manifest to insure that we don't "hit the wall." It has become our legacy to do so and become content to lie there in a crumpled heap. Yet, it is through these experiences that the quality of compassion will soften our hearts. They will provide the resilience to rise up and attack the wall again and again, until we finally break through. This is the only breakthrough that our souls seek - to transcend the barriers of separation and division, to emerge from the fog of self-delusion, to see ourselves and all things in the light of unconditional love, and to live out of our unlimited nature...our Godhood.

Toward this end, a host of events - produced by the quite often subliminal energies of our collective (un)conscious and out-pictured as disease, war, murder, rape, and all manner of mayhem - are manifesting. These events that are emerging to refocus our perspective, are at the crest of a wave of "inner change." Their aim is to nudge if not shock us into releasing our attachment to limited identity. Chief among their sponsors, script writers and producers are our tendencies toward fear, separation, and division. These are the energies that wrestle for dominance over our Being at the most subtle levels of our thought and feeling natures. When under their influence, it's not unusual for us to misinterpret and, quite often, infer the opposite of what the universe intends in its messages to us.

Quite often, our conventional ways of interpreting events - our penchant for labeling them "good or bad," "right or wrong" - inhibit our ability to see their value, hear their message and receive their gift at its highest potential. While change is imminent, the voices of fear and intimidation would have us skirting around and manipulating the external, while attempting to maintain the inner status quo. Reminiscing about the "good old days," and attempting to pray, legislate and regulate them back into existence, we fail to see the writing on the wall. Its message is simple and clear: "To comprehend the basis for the outer, we must look within. To change the outer, we must change within."

This change is not about whether or not we have prayer in schools. In fact, it's not about religion at all. In spite of all our prayers, platitudes and supplications, religion remains the favorite hiding place for our most secret sins, and the epitome of collective ego run amok. This emerging energy is geared to stripping away all of our pretense, so that we might come face to face with the unmitigated results of the highest and lowest expressions of our personal and collective creativity. This constitutes our only chance for bringing forth different results.

Our outer world is a reflection of our inner world. When we project our lack of self-love and acceptance onto others, we express dismay at those acts and images which defy our sense of the appropriate. With no qualms about inflicting injury or taking life to safeguard our interpretations of "right and wrong," we generate intense and confrontational energy around our "right to life" or "pro-choice" dogma. Yet, we are quick to disclaim responsibility when our collective zeal produces those who bomb clinics and murder doctors. Let's not forget our penchant for peering into the bedrooms of others to insure that their sexual conduct meets our approval. The result of meeting our disapproval is to be labeled a pervert, and be subjected to verbal condemnation, social ostricization and/or physical confrontation.

All the while, storms are brewing. The pattern of these storms defy convention, for they are showing up in places and at times that render our psychological almanacs and societal climatic charts useless. Their intensity is more severe than anything we've witnessed, and their destruction is - all at once - deeply profound and personal. The routine response in the face of a storm is to seek refuge in familiar surroundings. Yet, the storms that are blowing in to wash away the foundations of our illusory world are arising quickly, repeatedly and powerfully. Their unpredictable patterns make it not as expedient or desirable to retreat to the familiar comfort of old fallout shelters. Consequently, we are being divinely assisted with releasing ourselves from ongoing cycles of ignorance, pain, dismay, and heartbreak. We are being swept to a powerful point for beginning, in earnest, the work of purging ourselves of our tendencies toward limitation and conditional love and acceptance.

Due to the evolutionary point at which the planet has arrived, this purging process is occurring, to some extent, under its own power. The increased occurrences and intensity of what we call "natural disasters" are indicative of the Cosmic Intelligence of Mother Earth refuting the notion that She is merely a dumping ground for the by-products of humankind's folly. Bearing witness to some of the most extreme and devastating weather conditions in modern history, we are witnessing an intensified display of Earth's awesome ability for cleansing and self-restoration. Having remained faithful in her role as a life-sustaining entity, she is enforcing her right to survive and flourish by rebelling against an accumulative assault upon her natural estate. She has been made ill from toxins emitted by generations of unconscious, inconsiderate creativity. In her own way, with the aid of many conscious co-creators, she is saying "Give me liberty or give me death."

## The Crops of "Hybrid Seed"

One of the most profound effects these energy shifts are having on our individual lives is that our coveted senses of "security," "morality" and "truth" are being assailed. I saw a bumper sticker on a car on the highway yesterday that states it well. It said: "My karma ran over my dogma." I will change this just a bit to say that: "Our karma is overrunning our dogma." As a former Pentecostal minister operating in a totally different space in consciousness, I can really relate. What this says to me is that the seeds we have sown - via the energies projected into the ethers through our thoughts, fears, attitudes, words and deeds (both public and private) - are sprouting what I call "hybrid crops" or variant strains of the fruits of chaos and destruction.

There are many recent examples of this phenomenon. It is evident in the eighteen month spree of school shootings that resulted in multiple deaths and injuries across the nation, as well as two murder/suicides and police shootings (here in Atlanta), that exacted a tremendous toll of loss of life, physical injury and shattered dreams. Events such as these - and those which may be happening in your proximity - are so shocking to our dispositions that they have the effect of "knocking us out of the box of conventional interpretation." Though our predisposition toward old scripting and role-playing renders us quite willing to label the perpetrators "bad seed," all attempts at understanding their underlying motivations push us to the limits of our preconditioned interpretations. Faced with this inability to comprehend the depths of their human dilemma, we are, ultimately, cast into a psychological and emotional fog that thickens with each event.

Extensive media coverage has made us all familiar with the events which unfolded in the schools. Yet, peering through the fog of our delusion, no one saw the school shooting epidemic or these other events arising. There were no clear warning signs. Those who had the greatest exposure to these shooters had no clue that they were capable of such acts. They were, generally, considered to be "normal" if not "nice" individuals with no apparent proclivity toward such heightened levels of violence. One of the incidents that occurred in Atlanta involved a stepfather who awakened the household of seven other persons (five children and two adults) at approximately 6 am. He summoned them into one room, and there announced his intention to kill them all and proceeded to do so. A few minutes later, he took his own life. This account was given by the sole survivor, an eleven year old boy who, after being shot, escaped death by playing dead. This incident boggled the minds of all who knew the stepfather. According to all accounts, he was a very loving man - a "gentle giant" who spent a great deal of time playing with the children - a man who often volunteered as a chaperon for school field trips

These mass shootings in the Atlanta suburb of Buckhead provide another example of how - as the energy of transformation swirls, churns and forges a clearing through mass consciousness - its effect has become overwhelming to some. It is certainly incomprehensible to consider that a man could kill his wife (either before or after a Boy Scout meeting over which he presided as scout master), return home to kill his two children the following day and proceed to initiate an onslaught of injury, murder and suicide that reeked an historical level of local devastation. While a background check revealed evidence of a "suspicious" if not shady past, Mark O. Barton and the other leading characters in these deeply impacting and infamous acts were considered "normal and likable" individuals. Yet, there is a seemingly indescribable something that set them off on those particularly fateful mornings. As with similar incidents, that "something" has left its indelible imprint upon the community of human consciousness. The one thing this "hybrid" imprint has not left us is a clear sense of cause.

In that hosts of similar events are cropping up in communities around the globe, I share these incidents to illustrate how we are beginning to experience the emergence of a rash of events that don't fit the scripts we are accustomed to seeing. Engulfing and driving these experiences are the latent energies of our mental, emotional and psychological warfare, as well as our desire to remember our origin and oneness. And while we are not consciously aware that we are the source of the energy that drives this mayhem, it is indeed our collective consciousness that spurs, supports and reinforces these events.

There have always arisen those events which have awakened and stirred the deep yet latent reservoirs of compassion within our souls. As instruments of opportunity to both see ourselves more clearly and embrace our undeniable connection, their effect - though deeply impacting - is, most often, short-lived. Overcome by disbelief, shock and dismay, we are rendered emotionally incapable of looking beyond the individual events and the role players to seek out the procuring cause. It is much more expedient to isolate and label each perpetrator as someone who cleverly disguised his or her psychosis, or "slipped through the cracks." It is a far more challenging matter to discern our role in causing those fissures and to see just how wide and multiple those cracks are.

It's important to note that a history of emotional or mental instability is not a prerequisite to becoming "swept" into this whirlpool of transformational energy. All that is required is a proclivity toward fear, which leads to an affinity with anger, anxiety, depression, alienation, possessiveness, jealousy, hatred, greed, or any other lower emotional expression. The way we posture ourselves in relation to the events of our lives - often seeing ourselves as the "victim" of someone or something - is quite enough to draw us into a drama with magnanimous consequences. Edged out of a parking spot or cut off by someone attempting to merge into traffic, we fly into an emotional tirade that escalates into a phenomenon that we call "road rage." Who knows what ignited the spark for the individuals in the stories I shared? The one thing that is clear: in his own way, each of these individuals felt that this world - given its current configuration, consciousness and course - held little promise for reversing what appeared to be a downward spiral toward imminent demise. They abandoned all hope that they and - in some cases - their families would ever find inner peace and a lasting since of connection and purpose. This level of desperation is much more prevalent than you may think. It affects the young and old, rich and poor and the notable as well as the relatively unknown.

*Why the Children?*

> *"Tell me, can you see me in the faces of the children, in the eyes of your enemy - your friend?"*
>
> - I Come (A Song of Spiritual Renaissance) - Raja

If there is any consensus among us concerning how we might be most deeply aroused, it pertains to the welfare of our children. Their innocence, curiosity, hope, and zest for life remind us of how we used to be, as well as to where we might return to discover our true nature. We demonstrate great proficiency at shielding ourselves from the unfortunate plight of another adult. Yet, we have this unspoken protective instinct when it comes to the little ones. Therefore, the increased involvement of children in these highly traumatic events (as what we consider perpetrators and victims) is a source of grave concern. We ache at the thought of their little lives being "cut short." And, to appease our emotional distress and bewilderment, we assign their plight to the incomprehensible will of an unknown God.

Having taken great care in cultivating our "private gardens" of religious, financial, educational, and communal security, we desperately struggle to bolster ourselves, casting off the notion that we can be intimately affected, or that these events could happen in "our community." We respond publicly by sharing the grief and offering support to those most directly impacted. Yet, privately, we confront our difficulty with understanding the source of these dilemmas and dealing with them introspectively at all. Though deeply moved by their carnage, we are reluctant to share any responsibility for their existence. For doing so would require that we make a deeper inquiry into their cause. As mind-boggling manifestations of utter darkness, they remind us of the deep, dark places within ourselves, and seem to defy the very notion that we are a remotely civil people, not to mention civilized. As such, they afford an opportunity to distance ourselves even further from the light that is being cast upon our collective estate.

Our willingness to embrace such events as a gift would compel us to journey beyond societal interpretation to seek definitive answers from the "Source of all things." Our inquiry would prompt us to transcend the walls of our private gardens, where we have customarily passed our time skimming the surface of the soil. While applying more fertilizer to answers that have provided but pseudo relief, we are careful to avoid asking deeper, more probing questions. Though the equivalent of emotional bandages and gauze, our historical responses have done nothing to heal the withered saplings, which constitute our collective psyche. With no conscious awareness that we are the sowers who cast these seeds upon the soil (since they don't appear to be "after our own kind," we take a veiled responsibility for them - at best - and, consequently, receive little if any new insight into their cause. We opt instead for the mind-numbing conclusion that "God sure works in mysterious and unquestionable ways."

Yet when the children are involved, we have a much easier time bridging the gaps, crossing the boundaries and sharing each others' pain. As we probe our depths to consider what can be done to make this world a safer and more peaceful place, the pain tends to penetrate our consciousness and linger at much deeper levels. We feel that, in many ways, the children are our last bastion of hope. Speaking of them as "our future," we hold out great hope that they will somehow "save us," by finally getting what we have for so long failed to get. Consequently, at the behest of our collective souls, we are creating dramas that feature those souls who are our children in more prominent roles.

In a very real sense, our children are mirroring what they see and sense in greater society. Their actions are born of a spiritual dictate. They are not doing so by conscious design. Their resounding message to us is that they are present and significant now, and that they are observing what we are doing and being now. Though it seems that they don't honor our presence, be clear that it's not that they have a problem with what we do. Their problem seems to be with our lack of honesty about what we do and why we do it. As though laying their souls on the alter, they are saying, if there is to be any hope, we must see that their dramas are more honest, in your face interpretations of what we so cleverly and subtly propagate from behind the walls of our private gardens.

## *The Myth of "Private Gardens"*

Here is a basic, all-pervading reality that has been cleverly obscured through our altered-ego states and social indoctrination; a reality that is beginning to show up at our collective doorsteps: Despite all appearances to the contrary - within the realm of societal consciousness - there are no "private gardens." While we have access to an unlimited supply of seeds (creative thoughts) that we may sow privately, within the limited confines of social consciousness, there simply are no private gardens. Though some may reap more liberally than others and are quite often more selective as to what they put on their plates, there is but one cooperative garden to which we contribute the seeds of our collective consciousness. Along with all other sowers, we reap the harvest of their manifestation.

## Charting a Course for the New Millennium

It is true that we all have our individual lifetimes of assessment and evaluation (judgment) through which we filter our experiences. We do so in order to arrive at the perspectives upon which we build our lives. Yet, the fact remains that, at the root of it all, as the fertilizer for any and all seeds (creative thoughts) that we sow, rests either the energy of fear or the energy of love. These are the two basic energy cooperatives at work within our manifest reality. Our only chance for cultivating anything that resembles a private garden (for gaining sovereignty and peace) is to retrieve the inner knowledge that will enable us to free ourselves from the shackles of fear and limitation. This liberty, accompanied by an awareness of our true identity, can only be obtained by embarking the journey to Life-Mastery, which is the "Inner Path." This is a truth that the altered ego (the personification of every misguided human creation) has taken every measure imaginable to conceal from our conscious minds. As a diversionary tactic, through a ruthless usurpation of your creative imagination, it has sent you scampering out the back door in search of liberty and justice while your true guide to freedom and individual Life-Mastery stands knocking at the front. This altered self is armed with the understanding that your soul is engaged in the righteous pursuit of individual, Godly expression or the quest to master the principle of "separately but without separation." Consequently, through the use of fear, intimidation and deception - the altered ego has unduly harnessed this freedom instinct. Seeking fulfillment, it sends us marching onto the battlefields of worldly accomplishment with orders to subdue and conquer any and everything that we feel will give us a sense of identity (separateness) and power. After having explored our darkest nature - finding no real satisfaction, we return, time and time again, to the center of our being. It is there that we convalesce, seeking refuge and release from the stark terror visited upon our souls by the atrocities we've committed in blind pursuit of the elusive "meaning and purpose" for our lives. Yet, we descend - time and time again - to engage a parallel drama.

Our relentless pursuit of the trappings of the "surrogate kingdom of altered-ego" binds us to a cycle of illusion, heartbreak and dismay. As though primitive, prehistoric and unlearned, we continue to engage the same processes with little or no adjustment. Neglecting lifetimes of evidence to the contrary, we are convinced that this time - with the aid of advanced technology, a bustling economy and more cleverly devised schemes - "dis-may work."

## A Precursor to Every War

Every war that has ever been fought - every conflict that has led to bloodshed - has had at its core the notion of "mine versus yours." Whether the illusion centered around land ownership, the possession of other individuals (slaves, relationship partners, children, etc.) or political and/or religious ideology, the bottom-line has always been my "dogma" (my "am god" in reverse) versus yours. I'm reminded of a dog food commercial that has been popular over the years. It was put to music, sang by children, and went like this:

> "My dog's better than your dog. My dog's better than yours. My dog's better cause he eats Kennel Ration. My dog's better than yours." My dog's faster, etc., etc., etc.

Your altered-ego has, for ages, demonstrated that the best way to propagate a dogma within a society is to indoctrinate its children; and as you well know, we in the "Earth Theater Community" are quite clever at creating jingles to fuel the myth of separation. This unceasing campaign is played out daily through video game and movie violence and deprecating messages in music and other entertainment forms. The attitudes with which our children often engage competitive sports or see others engage them provides another opportunity to witness the indelible connection between wrestle mania and ego mania.

It's obvious that the initiator of any competition that gains its reward as the result of demeaning its competitor fails to grasp the undeniable truth of our connectedness. The relentless elbowing that signals our need to "position ourselves in the market" blinds us to the fact that we are, by cosmic design, joint recipients of the fruits of our collective consciousness. As such, what we send out into the collective ultimately "shows up on our plate," or comes back to visit us privately. Quite often, having added to itself the endorsement of other energies after its kind, it shows up with more pronounced vigor and greater resolve. The key to breaking this cycle is in understanding its pattern. Once clear, we can override its impact by plumbing our creative resources to discover ways to promote our products than by undermining someone else's.

The truth is that each of us has a right to be here. Our individual and collective talent and abilities are suited for the time and space we occupy. By adjusting our default demeanor from "I win you lose," to one where

## Charting a Course for the New Millennium

we honor the good of others as well as our own, we can begin to experience just how vast and expansive this universe of ours truly is. This is the way to manifest the vision we've glimpsed in our fleeting moments of conscious awareness. We have the blueprint. It is emblazoned upon our souls. We are the "Master Builders." This fact is evidenced time and time again by the way we are with one another when drawn together by what we see as tragedy and crisis. Yet, as though thick-headed and unable to comprehend, we muddle around confused and amazed at the results we get when we ignore the signs that point the failure to honor our connectedness.

To use a baseball analogy, it is as though we're poised at the plate - one at-bat after another - insistently waiting on a mid-speed fast-ball, right down the middle of the plate. As a matter of course, the energy of our collective consciousness is serving up a variable diet of curves, sliders, sinkers, breaking balls, with an occasional 100 m.p.h. fast ball at varying locations within the strike zone. As is the case with so many hitters who make their adjustments too late in the game, when the pitch we've been waiting for finally comes, we've given up on it. Lulled to sleep by a lack of engagement, we stand there frozen, and strike out. It often takes many trips to the plate and many strikeouts before we are able to get comfortable and focused enough to "pick up the rhythm of the pitcher." We are, then, able to anticipate more clearly and swing more freely, in opposed to "taking strikes," while waiting for our favorite pitch to come sailing down the middle of the plate.

We are ascending the realm of true Life- Mastery, freedom and Godhood. Anchoring this shift is the message that "the door has closed on the era of limitation, which encompasses both karma and dogma." The leap in consciousness that this portends is by no means an easy feat. It will require that you examine the ways you have become "fixed," and make a commitment to open yourself to a broader interpretation of life. In completing the journey, our "karma" (the fruits or life we've created through our limited thinking) may have to overrun our "dogma" (current perception of absolute truth) - at many levels, in many fashions time and time again, before we emerge from limited mind. The times we are experiencing provide our greatest opportunity for completing our quest for this breakthrough. The crucial nature of these times compels me to delve deeper beneath the surface of societal consciousness to continue 'ferreting out" the procuring cause of our collective dilemma.

## Fruit After Its Own Kind

The striking and deeply disturbing events that I refer to as "hybrid crops" also provide an opportunity to get beyond our judgments of who might be more prone to commit certain acts or express themselves in certain ways. They also have the potential to aid us in ascending our personal and collective hypocrisies. Events such as the shootings at Columbine High and other schools as well as the acts of domestic terrorism, are - at their core - a substantial gift from our collective consciousness. As utterly painful, impacting and costly as they were, these events are of major importance in helping us to break through the barriers of class and racial stereotyping. Yet, as is the case with many such gifts, when one factors in the anesthetic influences of mainstream interpretation, elapsed time and spiritual malaise, there is the threat that the deeper message may be lost.

Beyond the shock, disgust, disbelief and clouds of despair exists a tremendous opportunity to embrace a fuller expression of our humanity. They are also beneficial for bringing us to greater clarity about how destructive and all-pervasive these energies can be. When we (through our collective negligence, indifference and maliciousness) release less than righteous energy dynamics into the Universe, the devastation is relatively indiscriminate and all-encompassing. In spite of the pain we have suffered at the behest of these energies, we have not arrived at the point of purging their trace from our collective hearts. As venomous serpents, they have staked-out a comfortable existence. They lie tightly coiled at the heart-center of collective consciousness, prepared to strike out at anyone who disturbs their lair.

While my eyes are awash with the vivid colors of Godhood, I am clear that there are those who have committed their energies to promote social disease through race baiting, homophobia, class separation, financial disenfranchisement, and other tools of hatred and discord. Though often subtle in their expression, they have their chosen roles, and they play them well. While often deeply disguised and submerged beneath layers of pseudo acceptance and civility, these "ulterior energies" flow outward into the Universe lending their support to the agendas of the most vicious, pronounced social terrorists, "race-baiters" and "ethnic cleansers" on the planet. Such as societal consciousness is, and given the extent of disconnect that exists between the races, it's reasonable to say that the school shootings would not have caused such a ground-swell of shock, grief and/or controversy had they occurred in urban Detroit, Los Angeles or Atlanta. The level of expectation that is held out for urban youth is reflected in the sense that - given environmental considerations - certain things just don't occur in certain places, or among certain people. Yet, this statement that I repeatedly heard while visiting Littleton, Colorado hints to a reality that seeks our collective attention: "If it can happen here, it can happen anywhere."

*Crops of "Hybrid Seed" continued*

The word' 'hybrid" bodes well for casting light upon the Littleton Colorado incident as well as other events that are beginning to show up in our world. By definition, hybrid means "the offspring of genetically dissimilar parents or stock." I believe that given the racial and cultural consciousness that we inherit from our parents and ancestors, there is inherently nothing creatively different or separate about you, me, or anyone else who's trapped within the confines of societal consciousness. At this level of consciousness, we are, largely, the products of our environment. Even so, the deeper truth of our connectivity is age-old. Despite this truth, we've gone to great lengths to ignore any evidence of this connectivity. As a consequence, our ignorance and resistance have driven us deeper and deeper into the caves of isolation and fear. To support our dismemberment, we have created an illusion of separateness that out-pictures its own sustaining reality. Yet, as a member of the "co-op of collective consciousness," the same underlying energy (fear) that saturates the seeds you sow, impresses its identifying marker upon the genetic structure of all who suffer fear, without exception.

When we fail to seize the opportunities life presents to see ourselves as part of a unified force of God-awareness, our deeper descent into ignorance causes several dynamics to come into play. These dynamics work to manifest what I refer to as "hybrid crops." One result is that our sense of ourselves as "alienated" creates its own reality, replete with all the props. This "subjective reality" commingles with the "absolute reality" of who we are, as "co-creators in collective consciousness." These two dissimilar energies, working at cross purposes, bring forth what are, quite often, ugly, mutated offspring that resemble and reflect the energies of self-delusion, hypocrisy and fear, or the out-picturing of disparate and incongruent realities about who we are.

Quite often, our creations appear so downright frightening, monstrous, and deformed that we can't love ourselves or them enough to claim paternity. We have an even greater difficulty seeing the wonderful gifts they've brought to our lives. These gifts are the opportunity to gain absolute clarity about our creative nature and power, as well as the opportunity to see ourselves in others. In lieu of taking ownership, their lineage is attributed to the "devil," and their manifestation to the wrath of God or anything more convenient than our misguided use of Divine creativity. Thus, the spiral of disillusionment and pain cycles another round as we distance ourselves even farther from the truth.

Though we experience fleeting moments of compassion, connectivity, clarity, and truth, our escape and permanent refuge is sought within the comfortable confines of disclaim and disconnect. We are not yet willing to admit our culpability to ourselves; for to do so would require that we admit knowing that which we claim to have no knowledge of - Just how powerful we are by virtue of our connection with the Source. Yet, there is a lightening bolt of self-revealing truth born out of the scripture found in Matthew 7:20, which states: "Wherefore by their fruits ye shall know them."

## Toward "Conscious Change"

As is the nature of personal growth, the most expedient shifts occur when we are consciously aware of our right to choose, and choose to be proactive with our creative energies rather than reactive. This is our opportunity in this moment. In order to align with the movement that is occurring, the fences must come down. And they will come down, one way or another. We can consciously remove them by identifying and eliminating blockages of fear, false perception and hatred of self and others, or we can continue to allow the energies of fear, separation and division to prompt our growth. If we choose to become more accepting of ourselves and each other, we can bring our current stage-play to full circle, and awaken to our truly divine selves. In truth, we are beings who love to love and share our light. Yet our conditioning and indoctrination have rendered us unwilling to express this innate nature for our own nurturing. This conditioning also circumvents our ability to project it onto others for their healing, or to honor this innate quality in others.

The time has come to realize that, in essence, there is no "me" that is separate from "you." It is time for those of us who profess a spiritual

## Charting a Course for the New Millennium

understanding to examine our lives for the ways that we inadvertently reinforce the divisive energies of alienation, condescension and superiority. We would do well to search our secret thoughts, attitudes, feelings, and actions for subconscious pockets of fear; and to consciously choose to release them to love. It is time for us to become what we say we desire to see - fearlessness, fairness, freedom, and oneness. It's time for those who stand for humanity and its preservation to "Walk in the light that we might have fellowship, one with another[1]."

We might begin by asking ourselves if - in pursuit of a comfort zone for harboring our narrow opinions of right and wrong, life-style preferences and other pet peeves - we have divided the "One Mind of Cosmic Consciousness" into comfortable cliques that we call "like-minded individuals." When we decide that we have ascended above other God-beings on the basis of race, nationality, spiritual awareness, financial well-being, education, job status, or any other reason, and begin to treat them as "less than," it's good for us to be re-minded that "pride goeth before destruction and a haughty spirit before a fall[2]." It is just such a spirit - regardless of how cleverly disguised or ignorantly engaged - that sponsors, underpins and reinforces all human discord.

From fundamental religionists rallying the "elect of God" to confront and convert a world of "sinners" to "New Thought" congregants who speak of being "recovering fundamentalists" who long to convert their less enlightened fellows to their higher point of view, the energy dynamics are the same - "separation and division," "my dogma (am god) versus yours." From our children dissing schoolmates because they see them as outcasts who don't fit established cliques, to our cringing at the thought of picking up a hitchhiking stranger, the energy dynamics are the same - "fear and isolation."

An accounting of the cause of all great historical atrocities would reveal the presence of these energy dynamics anchored at their root. From the prehistoric territorial battles between cavemen Og and Grogg, and the conflict which caused Cain to slay Abel over their godly sacrifices, to the cunning deception of Jacob, which afforded him the perks of the firstborn intended for his brother Esau, on through the elimination of him who was called "King of the Jews," you can find their imprint. The Spanish Inquisition and "Christian" Crusades, World Wars 1 and 2,

1   1 John 1:7
2   2 Proverbs 16:18

the Vietnam conflict, and the assassinations of Presidents Lincoln and Kennedy, Robert Kennedy and Martin Luther King Jr. all bear the mark of a strong resistance to confirming our oneness. Beneath every personal and collective conflict we create and justify on a daily basis rests spiritual blindness, induced and reinforced by fear and guilt infested religious, social and political dogma.

At the risk of appearing an overly optimistic idealist, I submit that the ships that have brought us to our current port of social interaction are on fire and sinking fast. Few social and theological prognosticators or the most common thinkers among us would disagree that we have fallen - i.e. that mass consciousness currently exists in a clearly primitive state of spiritual/social awareness and interaction. Most would agree that despite our technological sophistication and its potential for closing the geographical gap between peoples and cultures, the "dog eat dog" manner in which we customarily anticipate, receive and engage each other not only persists, but has intensified.

The tone of our business practices, advertising campaigns, civil and religious politics, and the way we routinely settle personal, community, and global disputes does not bode well for our claim as a highly advanced society. They are clear signs that our hearts have waxed cold, and that we are due for a little "global warming." This global warming is exactly what is occurring within the hearts of those who seek it.

> *"I want to know when the killing will end, on our streets and across the sea. Please understand, we've got to love our fellowman and learn to live in harmony."*
>
> - Anytime We Come Together (A World Anthem) - Raja

At first glance, the prospect for sweeping change appears bleak. Yet, it is our collective task to build fleeter, more utilitarian vessels to transport us to our next greatest good. To facilitate this process, a "reordering of cosmic energy" has created a space of realignment. Many are following the urge to make choices that will aid them in uncovering buried aspects of their higher nature. This nature, humanitarian spirit, love essence, or "God-fire" is the key to tapping the energy of Spiritual Genius. It is the inspiration that prepares the way for the manifestation of "the substance of things long awaited and hoped for." It is the energy that can and will propel us forward in leaps and bounds of self-awakening, soul restoration and global healing.

# Charting a Course for the New Millennium

An important question for this time is: Do we choose to take this leap forward in our pursuit of humanity and personal liberty, or do we continue to grovel for dollars and physical dominion by beating down those most vulnerable to exploitation and manipulation? Given the direction I feel our hearts yearn for, it's my prayer and belief that focusing our energy to sustain the current primitive level of political/social/economic interaction - which features political posturing, class separation and a "survival of the fittest mentality" - will cease to be our choice.

Though our pace has been somewhat slow, we are poised at a pivotal point of "graduation" to a higher level of personal and collective integration. Having peered beyond the veil to glimpse a world that has shed the constraints of division, unhealthy competition and war, I have an undaunted belief that we have arrived at a pivotal point for change. The underlying question for us, as individuals, is whether we arrive at this point by conscious choice or forced by unmitigated circumstance. I am aware of those who feel that integration is not necessarily a good thing. My response is that a sincere quest for your true identity will rid you of the illusion that race constitutes your highest identifier. As we move forward to embrace a true sense of our collective humanity, this shift will call forth new and broader perspectives on what constitutes community.

A friend in Canada sent me the following information, which grants a view of the world through a more panoramic and, at the same time, a more condensed lens than most are accustomed to. Compiled in 1989 by Dr. Phillip M Harter, MD it states that: If we could shrink the earth's population to a village of precisely 100 people, with all the existing human ratios remaining the same, it would look something like the following. There would be:

- 57 Asians
- 21 Europeans
- 14 from the Western Hemisphere, both north and south
- 8 Africans
- 52 would be female 48 would be male
- 70 would be nonwhite 30 would be white
- 70 would be non-Christian 30 would be Christian
- 89 would be heterosexual

- 11 would be homosexual
- 6 people would possess 59% of the entire world's wealth and all 6 would be from the United States.
- 80 would live in substandard housing
- 70 would be unable to read
- 50 would suffer from malnutrition
- 1 would be near death; 1 would be near birth
- 1 (yes, only 1) would have a college education
- 1 would own a computer.

When one considers our world from such a compressed perspective, the need for acceptance, understanding and education becomes glaringly apparent.

In a global sense, maintaining an effective role in world leadership will require America to move beyond an "entice them with dollars or persuade them with bombs" diplomacy. Its leaders will be charged with elevating the standard for fair, diverse, and compassionate representation or relinquishing the leadership role. Alignment with the energy of this shift will require a balancing of the energies of the ego and the heart - a balancing of the masculine and feminine aspects of our beings. This would require that the status quo, Caucasian male dominated, "good-o-boy," country club structure of "pork barrel politics" that currently charts our course be reordered. I believe that this shift is already occurring. As a result of an inner call for more conscious leadership, I foresee a significantly different brand of leader emerging to engage all areas of human interaction. Men and women from varied walks of life are being drawn forward to aid in redefining how we interact with each other locally and globally. To further facilitate the process, the laws governing campaign financing could use some restructuring to make high political office more accessible to a wider range of candidates. This idea has met perennial resistance from career politicians who have become comfortably entrenched in their "well paid for" jurisdictions. Their overblown war chests and partisan gerrymandering policies provide a certain guarantee of control over electoral results.

On a more interactive level, taxpayer tolerance for having untold resources squandered during session after grid-locked session of biased bickering will one day reach its summit, and this displeasure will be reflected at the ballot box. At a yet deeper level, having had our senses of national and personal security shaken by terrorist attacks upon the New York Trade Center, Oklahoma City Federal Building and Olympic Park, we have come to see that we are by no means immune to covert attacks from those whom we have fashioned as our enemies. Our down home experience with the carnage of terrorism will cause us to become less tolerable of the covert incidents abroad that we have unwittingly underwritten with our tax dollars.

Ministers whose overblown senses of self, and messages of God as a "hater of humans and our ways" will find few - if any - congregants to fill their pews and pockets. Our ears - having become more sensitive to inner guidance - will not accept messages of hatred and division along any lines or from any source. On our journey toward self-recovery, having our ears open to hear clearly, we will stand up, confront and adamantly refuse to support those supposed "universal truths" that ring discordant within our souls. Having severed the umbilical cord of fear and released our willingness toward being persecuted, guilt-ridden and psychologically pimped, we will boldly proclaim and honor ourselves as source, and yield to none but the guidance that emanates from our newly awakened hearts.

The painful process of learning (remembering) to listen to our hearts will bring us to the point of having grown tired of presumed enemies and war. Consequently, we will refrain from electing politicians who are war-mongers...locally or abroad. We will, instead, opt for leaders who are less prone to engage their hawkish instincts at a whim. With fear taken out of the equation, we will see God in the eyes of those we presumed our enemies, as well as those whom we know to be our friends. It is then that we will come to see and know who God truly is.

We are becoming sensitized to the fact that the pain experienced by a mother or father in Kosovo, Serbia, Rwanda or Iraq who has lost a son or daughter to the alter-ego driven madness of a "superpower agenda" is no less dire than the pain experienced by a parent who has lost a child to a school shooting in Littleton, Colorado, Paducah, Kentucky, Pearl, Mississippi, or Jonesboro, Arkansas. Becoming fully awakened to this reality will cause us to vote for leaders with a more compassionate balance between heart and head. Candidates whose greatest attributes are their campaign war chests and ability to speak undermining and scandalous rhetoric about their "opponents" will spend their millions but will not be chosen as our representatives. Lacking the sense that the energy of war (even at the level of political campaigning) is a cosponsor of the war that breaks out in our schools, on our streets and across the sea they, too, will draw to themselves the opportunity to experience the heartbreak (heart-wake) that money and/or influence cannot circumvent or heal. This is the level of awakening that our current state of consciousness often requires to bring about change.

As we awaken to the inherent connection that exists among us, those who seek to continue administering mouth to mouth resuscitation to these "dying paradigms of societal consciousness" (religious, political or otherwise) will find themselves of little to no use in the universal scheme of things. Absent the willingness to change, and unable to breath the enlightened air of a newly emergent consciousness, they will have served their purpose and will move on.

## Rising to the Occasion

We are marching, steadfastly, toward the "critical mass" (combined energy field) needed to invoke these changes. Those who are committed instruments of peace and unity (those who are delivered from the illusions of societal consciousness and are empowered to serve) are determined to see these changes occur in our lifetimes. So the bar has been raised and the obstacles are being removed. We are clear that an inability to cultivate a healthy sense of self-worth is behind our inability to value and respect others. Operating from the understanding that in order to "see it," you've got to "be it," we have doubled our determination to walk in the light of our own Self-knowing, and project the energy of Self-love into the world. Consequently, in this world of duality, opposing forces - subtle and otherwise - have also intensified.

Yes, despite a desire to trust that everything is beautiful and lovely, there are deeply entrenched, disagreeable forces with a vested interest in, at least, maintaining the status-quo. These forces are quite adept at manipulating the thought and feeling natures of mass consciousness. Yet, as conflicting and disjointing as it may appear, this duality is useful in moving us toward a synthesis in our quest for a conscious, unified field of oneness. As we experience more increasingly disruptive and unsettling events, our choice to utilize the energies of empathy and understanding to seek resolution through conscious creative action will bring many into the awakening of their "true selves." Your heart is the pathway to this awakening.

Absent the compulsion to acquiesce to those who currently hold sway and resist a peaceful coexistence among all of creation, we will make the conscious choice to lend our energy toward shifting the paradigm. As a result of hearts being awakened and transformed, as masses of die hard constituents of alter-ego-centered division and separation consciousness die off, the meek will truly inherit the Earth. Having served their purpose, these discordant souls will exit the planet...job well done... end of story line.

To effectively serve in this new age of spiritual awareness and participate in creating a new world, you must redouble your personal commitment to spiritual growth. Be mindful that the energy that is blowing in to renew our souls can neither be defined by nor rest within the confines of "New Thought" or "God hasn't said anything new in 2000 years" fundamentalist religion. It flows directly from the Source into the brave and yearning hearts of earnest seekers. If you are willing to listen to Its voice, the Breath of Life will fill your heart with a boundless resource for renewing your Spirit and piercing the veil of false perception. It is here (beyond the veil) that you will come face to face with your Divine Nature or personal Genius.

The path to life transformation, true spiritual empowerment and conscious change is an inner path. It is a "heart path" more so than a "head path." Your ability to open your heart has very little to do with the power of your intellect, how many books you've read or how long you have been "on the path." It is a simple matter of your willingness to ascend beyond your boundary laden comfort zones to risk a ride on the unlimited, uncharted winds of the Divine. In essence, there is really nothing that you have to do. You are simply required to master the art of becoming. The adjustments are internal. The external comes into alignment as you follow your inner promptings.

The benefits of participation are never garnered at the expense of others, i.e. by beating others down or winning at the expense of someone else's supposed loss. They flow from a universal Source that is no respecter of persons. To provide them space, you must ascend above race consciousness, with its hatred inducing dramas, national and cultural egotism and all other alliances that promote an "us versus them" mentality. You must be willing to break from the herd and forget what you think you know about God, yourself and others, so that the Spirit of Universal Truth can renew your mind. You must "come off the page," "out of the book" and into an interactive life based on mutual respect, love and honor. You must release your skepticism, rise above victim thinking, affirm your unlimitedness, and fearlessly confront any appearances to the contrary. You will, then, become empowered to take responsibility for creating a life after your own heart's desire...believing that the Universe supports your efforts.

There is truth being spoken in your heart in this very moment. It is for you to muster the courage to show up, listen and trust its authenticity. The result will invariably be that you discover a richness of true identity that will redefine how you see yourself, interact with others and move forward in the world from this day forward. These courageous steps will allow you to make connection with that which is never vulnerable and can never be hurt or damaged. This Spirit of Life and Love (the "All-knowing God-Self") which dwells within you is the reality of who you are. It is the "core truth" of your Being. Your commitment to ascend beyond limited mind is the key to connecting with your true identity.

*Recovering Your Genius*

It is said that the average individual utilizes between twenty-five percent (25%) and thirty-five percent (35%) of his or her potential brain power. As individual energy fields with distinct and uniquely developed qualities or qualifications, we are being urged to purge ourselves of the dis-empowering energy that fosters these limitations. This is the key to opening those regions of the brain that are receptive to the higher vibrations of Mastery and Genius. Upon doing so, we will align with a universal energy flow that supports the use of these unique qualities to bring forth a new social/spiritual consciousness. This Genius is the key to mastering the seeming paradox of being "separate but without separation." The ability to comprehend the true implications and parameters of this "divine autonomy" is vital to your quest to establish your righteously sovereign kingdom of individual God expression.

I intentionally use the word "Genius" rather than talent to emphasize that I am speaking to more than aptitude and/or skill. While we all have wonderful gifts and talents, without the guidance of intuitive wisdom, the satisfaction we derive from exercising them as well as their impact and import for the world at-large is most often nominal. As we release limited ideas about ourselves, our worthiness, our potential, and the potential of others and begin to avail ourselves to the intuitive guidance of the "inner path," we will begin to open heretofore blocked regions of our brains. Consequently, we will bring forth the ideas and inventions that are key to our quest to redefine the nature of human interaction. Operating at this level of consciousness will render the current ideas of "majority," "minority," "superiority," and even "affirmative action" completely obsolete. Having arrived at the point of actively affirming who we are, the unleashing of this inner Genius will propel us to unparalleled heights of heartfelt creative expression and Life-Mastery.

While to some the word genius implies nothing more than extraordinary intellectual power as measured by one's performance on some standardized intelligence test, a high IQ, presumed brilliance or a special proclivity in a particular area of endeavor does not imply a connection with this inner Genius. As offspring of the Creator of the Universe, its meaning goes far beyond intellectual prowess, high proficiency or skill. Genius resides within each of us as a dynamic, revolutionary, spiritually inherent, and central part of our makeup. Residing at the "seat of our soul," it is our guide to wholeness, as it radiates a sense of Mastery, balance and true empowerment in all aspects of life.

This Genius holds the key to your individual contribution to the building of the collective Kingdom of heaven on earth. It is also your pathway to joy, self-fulfillment and peace. It holds the key to mastering every malady that will ever confront your life. This Genius has as its primary aim the rediscovery and unfoldment of the authentically empowered "transcendental you." Your task, birthright and destiny are to align with this Master Dishwasher, and allow it to guide you along the path to the unfolding of your greatest vision for yourself, your loved ones and your world.

Sir Francis Galton[3], a 19th-century British scientist, used the word genius to designate creative ability of an exceptionally high order, demonstrated by actual achievement. It involves originality, creativeness and the ability to think and work in areas not previously explored and, thus, to give the world something of value it would not otherwise

---

3    Hereditary Genius (1869)

possess. He formulated the theory that Genius is a very extreme degree of three combined traits: intellect, zeal and the power of working. This definition of Genius aids in setting the stage for the process that is "The Tao of Dishwashing - Tasking a Master Soul."

As you engage your pursuit of "life outside the box of societal indoctrination," take note that the move from mediocrity to true Mastery requires that you follow the guidance of your inner Genius as it flows through your willing mind. To enlist its aid, you must demonstrate your desire to be free. You must heed the inner calls to "wake up," "show up" and "own-up." Once you are awakened, conscious and truly present, you will be compelled to examine who you are (how you see yourself in the world), that you might make the leap from altered-ego identity to becoming grounded in your true nature.

The discovery and acceptance of your "true self is the first step in learning to listen to and follow the desires of your heart. It is at the root of these desires that the foundation of your unique kingdom will be discovered. Upon its discovery, you will be required to assess your commitment to being in integrity with its dictates. You must search your heart for the motivation beneath your desires, as well as for the actions you are willing to take in pursuit of their fulfillment.

Finally, you will be guided to the path that will provide direct passage to a new level of self-awareness and the unfolding of your dynamic destiny. This is the path of passion. Placement of your feet upon this path requires that you make a commitment to bringing zeal and passion to bear in all of your creative pursuits. By doing so, you liberate yourself from the bondage of mediocrity and fear (the perennial campgrounds of collective consciousness), thereby freeing your soul to ascend to true Mastery in all aspects of your life. The ultimate payoff is the discovery and alignment with the highest nature of your dynamic destiny and a conscious role in shaping the new world.

The path to preparing your soul for life mastery is a personal journey. Whether you ultimately engage the "Master Dishwasher" (spiritual guidance) and enlist Its aid depends upon your willingness to conquer your fears; for you can be certain that you will meet them along the path. You will also undoubtedly incur criticism from those whose fears have made them comfortable with the status-quo or too afraid to challenge it. You must, therefore, be willing to walk alone. At critical points you will do just that. Yet, you will have to be determined to embrace and, thereby, master whatever you encounter. Your commitment to apply passion to each of your creative expressions will, at the very least, lead to a rewarding and fulfilling life.

It is important to reiterate that your personal effort lends a great amount to the overall team objective. Only you, through the releasing of your fears and prior conditioning, can schedule the place and time for beginning your march toward freedom. In the way of encouragement, I say to you that the place is right where you are, and the time is now! You can make the connection. So, seize the day! Release any attachment to outmoded, dis-empowering social/spiritual paradigms, and see yourself and others in the light of a newly dawning age.

Here we are in one of the early contests of the twenty-first century. This is our long-awaited chance to capture the energy of a deeply defining moment, and emerge victorious as the power hitters we were born to be. It's the bottom of the ninth. We are the home team, and this is our biggest game to date. Facing a team called "Altered-Ego" from a place called "False-Self," we are down by three runs. You are at the plate with the bases loaded, two outs and a 3-2 count. Adjusting and altering how you view the "curves," "bad breaks," "sinkers," and "slides" of life (what you have come to accept as "truth and value," "right and wrong," "good and bad" in yourself and others) has afforded you an opportunity to connect with what is really going on, and to take a responsible role in healing your life and creating the world you desire to see. While comfortably establishing a rhythm for your bat, you've assumed your stance and dug-in. The pitcher is winding up. He stares in at you with that intimidating gaze. The ball is on its way to the plate. Here's the pitch! Swing Batter!!

## *Summary*

- Deeply impacting, worldwide change is occurring as we move into and through the new century.

- The often unsettling effects of these changes are being felt within our private and collective worlds.

- One effect is evidenced by an increased pursuit of self-knowledge and spiritual awareness.

- What we usually term "negative" events can be seen as positive stimulants for change.

- Each of us maintains the responsibility for creating our individual and collective worlds.

- Our thoughts, emotions, feelings, attitudes, words and deeds (both hidden and revealed) shape our perspectives, which - in turn - create the world we experience.

- The Universal Law of Attraction maintains that "Like attracts Like."

- Operating from a consciousness of fear draws us to those things we fear personally, and Charting a Course for the New Millennium contributes to creating the frightful things that show up in our world.

- Mass or "collective" consciousness is held captive and controlled by the energies of fear and divisiveness, as well as the presumed need for self-defense.

- All who suffer fear cast fear seeds into the garden of collective consciousness, and reap the fruits thereof. In this sense, there are no "private gardens."

- Your alter ego, supported by the energies of self-delusion and fear, has created an image of you as separate. This false image has fostered a descent into insecurity, disconnectedness and distrust.

- Hybrid crops are those shockingly unfamiliar events and circumstances that show up, unexpectedly, on our plates. They are born of the combined creative energies of our illusory, separate selves and who we truly are as co-creators in collective consciousness.
- There are "individuals" in this present-day world who have liberated themselves from the bondage of societal indoctrination. These individuals have come into an awareness of their Godhood.
- These awakened giants will spearhead a new brand of leadership that will demonstrate a truer balance between the head and the heart.
- We all have a unique destiny and "calling." It is an aspect of your destiny to discover your Godhood, and use this awareness to aid in shifting the energy of this planet to attract more life-enhancing outcomes for our future.
- Your willingness to walk the "inner path" of intuitive guidance will lead to the discovery of your spiritual genius.

# Chapter 2

*Who Am I? - The Dilemma of Personal Identification*

*"The task is to define oneself, for oneself in a manner that enables a relationship to oneself. In doing so, one becomes who one truly is."*

...Dr. Allan W. Anderson

    It seems that most people today live lives that are focused almost exclusively in the outer world. Who we are (how we see ourselves) is generally summed up by virtue of a not always subtle and never healthy subconscious "point system." We are literally driven by the things we feel we have to do to maintain an image manufactured by some outside source to whom we have surrendered definitive power.

    It has become our nature to construct a matrix into which we pour our socially oriented values. Assigning: 10 points for excellent credit; minus 10 if you've been bankrupt; add 15 points if you're married; (deduct 5 for each marriage beyond 1); if currently divorced, deduct 10; deduct an additional 20 if you are single and non-celibate; factor in your education, by institution and degree; add X number of points for your income, IQ. and, by all means, race. With Caucasian representing the standard, deduct, deduct, deduct if you are anything but!

    **\*\*** *Personal footnote: The race-related point deduction factor depends entirely on your personal level of self-esteem. If your bent is toward racial superiority, for your own personal gratification, you may want to add a few points.*

Once compiled, to arrive at an initial assessment of how you stack up in the world of societal consciousness, the data must be weighed against your particular demographic. Even with religion factored in, we literally worry ourselves into hell attempting to measure up to some superficial standard that is of no importance whatsoever to our souls.

    So who indeed are we? When asked this question, most folk (depending on when and where encountered) couch their answer in terms of myriad tags we hang on ourselves. Hardly, if ever, does the question prompt an answer that transcends race, nationality, gender, occupation, marital status, church membership, social affiliations, or other roles we play. In reality, this makes about as much sense as joining the community theater and transposing the character we play onto every aspect of our lives. Becoming obsessed with the role, we wear the costume and quote the script by rote, giving no attention to the unique opportunity life has given us to be perpetually self-generating in every moment of our lives. In the meantime, an incessant appeal resonates from the center of our being. It is our spirit beckoning us to remember from whence we have fallen. Its appeal to us is that we undress (pull off the costume), and return home to our authenticity.

> *"I had a ticket on a merry-go-round, jaded life, time was winding down. The roles that I played had run their time, and I knew I had hills to climb."*
>
> ...The Voices of Change - Raja

A common plight in today's society is that, absent a spiritual focus that encourages independent self-observation and introspection, we continue to limit ourselves to our ego based interpretations of who we are. Be it "African American male," "Reverend Smith," "Sue in accounting," "mom," or "the cable guy." our highest level of identification becomes our most treasured label. In a desperate attempt to find meaning and purpose for our lives, we cling to these labels, which oblige us to constantly worry about the mundane. "How's my credit?" "What kind of job evaluation will I receive?" "Do my children think I'm a good parent?" "Is my spouse having an affair?" If so, "What does that say about me?" "Do the neighbors like my flower bed," etc. etc. etc? All the while, the One who knows our true spiritual design patiently beckons us to counsel.

There are times and circumstances born of basic responsibility when it is appropriate for us to be concerned about how we show up in the world. Yet, in the midst of our concerns, there is a simple and largely neglected truth that our spirit would have us remember: "We are in this world, but not of it!"

# The Dilemma of Personal Identification

*Through the Eyes of a Child*

> *"...and a child shall lead them."* Isaiah 11:6

As a boy of 4 or 5, I was very much in touch with this mystery of "dual citizenship." While I did not have the ability to explain what I knew, my mother recently reminded me of my ability to "see beyond the veil." Quite often, I witnessed spirits or what we called ghosts walking through our house in broad daylight. I didn't know their identity then, nor do I now. I do know that, each time I asked my mother if she saw that man or woman who just walked through the living room, it literally scared the hell out of her. You see, like most folks, momma and I believed in but wanted nothing to do with ghosts. Even so, these experiences stimulated my early thinking about God, purpose and the unseen worlds. They also sponsored my childhood habits of sleeping with my head under the covers and wetting the bed... habits I maintained for quite awhile. Afraid of what or whom I might encounter on the path to the rest room, I just wasn't getting up in the middle of the night - no way - period!

Where our spirituality is concerned, sleeping with our heads under the cover has been popular for sometime. Fearful of looking beyond conventional explanations for our existence, we refuse to spend time alone with ourselves - going within listening to our own hearts. Unsure of whom and/or what we will encounter along the inner path, we settle for the rhetoric of someone whom we suppose knows the needs of our soul better than we. In essence, we opt for "dining out," rationalizing that, though we may not really like the food, at least, there will be no dishes. As a consequence, the extent of our estrangement from the higher part of ourselves is such that we are neither aware of Its existence nor attuned to Its activity.

Though we appear to chart the course of our own lives, there is a part of us that deliberately overshadows our agendas in order to work Its purpose. That part of our being, which we call "Spirit," works through our souls to move us toward Life Mastery and Spiritual Genius. If we were to accept the invitation to sit in counsel with our Spirit, we would avail ourselves to a vista of information about the true nature of human existence, as well as our personal path to Mastery. Our desire to know our true identity and purpose would spark a remembrance far beyond the limitations of physicality, personality and the roles we play.

Honoring ourselves enough to "show up" would reveal that it is we (made in the image and likeness of God) who chose this adventure into the "Earth Theater Community" (ETC as I refer to it)[4] as a path to experience the vastness of the kingdom, while simultaneously expanding its boundaries. When we limit our view to the exclusive use of "adult vision," we develop nearsightedness, and forfeit our ability to see beyond the appearances of the physical world. Yet, if we would look, again, through the eyes of a child, the veil would be lifted and we would see in our hearts that in which our souls delight most: "the key to the kingdom," our "true purpose" and "the springboard to Mastery and Genius in our lives." The resultant understanding of life's core agenda would place us at a powerful vantage point for understanding the events of our lives from a more empowering perspective. Taking time out to be alone with ourselves provides a space for washing away the film of limited perception; allowing us an opportunity to "see through a dark glass clearly."

Are you willing to show up, remove the blinders and surrender your false sense of self in lieu of rediscovering your true identity? Are you willing to look again, with childlike wonder, for the key to your unique kingdom? As it is said, in Luke 18:17 of the King James Bible: "Verily I say unto you, whosoever shall not receive the kingdom of God as a little child shall in no wise enter in." Remember, it is the children's innocence, curiosity, hope, and zest for life that remind us of how we used to be, as well as to where we might return to discover our true nature.

The following information will provide an opportunity for gazing within to consider your level of affinity with social consciousness. This will provide you the basis for making a clear choice to cut the chords that make you susceptible to societal manipulation; bonds that prohibit you from embracing a more authentic connection to your reason for being in the world.

---

4   ETC., short for et cetera, is also an acronym I devised for Earth Theater Communityl. As I view planet Earth to be an arena to which we descend to work out issues of soul growth and evolution, the word et cetera refers to our penchant for becoming enmeshed in a perpetual cycle of illusory sideline dramas..

The Dilemma of Personal Identification

*Social Consciousness Checklist*[5]

Check the following emotional switches, buttons and programs. Any time you are switched ON to these feelings, you are living in limited mind.

- Check your Doubt switch; turn OFF your doubt of everything, everyone, and self.
- Is your limitedness switch on? Turn OFF everything that you think you (and others)[6] are not.
- Check your hate button; flip it from standby to OFF.
- Set your Bitterness button to OFF; the past is the past.
- War switch to OFF; war is simply war with self.
- Disease switch to OFF; you don't need the identity anymore.
- Unhappiness switch to OFF; grab your joystick and prepare to take off to Flight level Super-Consciousness.
- Misery switch; flip it from standby to OFF - (though misery loves company)[7] who needs misery?
- Judgment of Others program; for effortless flight, reprogram to Love of Others program.
- Turn the Living for Others and Dying for Others program to OFF. This is the living to please the whole of the world who shan't ever be pleased program.

Your emergence from social consciousness - with its energy-zapping expectations and role-playing - into the unlimited realms of Super Consciousness and Genius will require that you make an honest and continual in-depth inquiry into how you are choosing to show up in the world.

---

5   Taken fron Destination Freedom A Time-Travel Adventure by Ramtha and Douglas Mahr - Prentice Hall Press 1989.
6   The portion in parenthesis is my addition.
7   The cliché in parenthesis is my addition.

## *Summary*

- A common tendency is to feel compelled to maintain an image manufactured by some outside source, to whom we have surrendered our power.
- Our often desperate attempts at finding meaning and purpose for our lives mire us in a pattern of limiting ourselves to ego-based identities.
- These identities are based on the roles we play rather than who we truly are.
- Sleeping with our heads beneath the covers (within the confines of habit and convention) signifies a fear of embarking the inner path of true self-discovery.
- A commitment to "showing up" to spend time alone going within to listen to your own heart will open a vista of spiritually enriching information about your true nature, origin and destiny.
- Our true identity is that of Spiritual Beings engaged in a "human adventure."
- We chose this adventure into (ETC) the Earth Theater Community as a way to simultaneously experience and expand its parameters; through expanding our perception of the potential possibilities.
- With childlike wonder, you can search the recesses of your heart for the key to your uniquely distinguished Kingdom.

A-Task: Make a list of the myriad of titles you use in defining yourself. Examine them for the value they bring to your experience. Now, allow your memory and imagination to take you back to those times when you felt most free and uninhibited by the roles you play. As a child, who did you imagine you would become? Consider how reconnecting with this time of childlike wonder might help you to release the pressure associated with the roles you play, and recover the inspiration and vitality we often sacrifice when we choose to view the world through the exclusive use of "adult vision."

# Chapter 3

*Showing Up: In Pursuit of "The Kingdom"*

*"The real voyage of discovery consists not in seeking new landscapes but in having new eyes."*

- Marcel Proust

One of my favorite personal history stories was related to me by my mother. She shared how, while at the hospital on the night of December 31, 1953, she was in the throes of major labor pain, preparing to sponsor her second child into the world. A "big headed baby boy" she called me. Any woman with this experience and those of us with at least a tad of empathy will agree that this is not an event to be prolonged. Yet, this is exactly what happened. According to momma, after many hours of arduous labor, the time arrived for me to debut. She was certainly ready but there was a problem - the nurses and doctor were not.

Much as is the case today, a great deal of hoopla and quite a few perks were bestowed upon the parents of the first infant born in the New Year. With the clock approaching midnight, the hospital crew conspired to have the first recorded birth occur at Barberton Citizens Hospital. So, according to mom, the nurses literally held her legs together while she screamed, cursed and threatened their lives, until 12:01 AM January 1st 1954 - the time I chose to "show up."

## The Nurse's Role

I certainly understand both sides of the drama that unfolded that night. My mother's position? - She had an idea (me) that she desired to give birth to, so that she could enjoy its fruit and the pain of carrying it around could begin to subside. The nurses, on the other hand, held the idea of delayed gratification. They reasoned that a few extra moments of birthing pain (which may have seemed years to momma) were worth the broader benefits associated with delaying my arrival. What neither of them was consciously aware of is that I, the spiritual part of that baby boy, was orchestrating the whole of these events from beyond the veil. My reason for sharing this story is that, despite what may appear to be an act of insensitivity by the hospital staff, I find in these events a bit of humor and a profound parallel to the challenges encountered, as we seek to "show up" and engage the path that leads to our life purpose. At the level of soul, beyond the whims of ego gratification, each of us has a clear understanding of what will bring wholeness and contentment to our lives. While lacking sufficient insight to consciously comprehend it for ourselves or explain it to others, the fact that we awaken each morning is testament that this reality continues to reside within our soul, seeking manifestation and radiating - if but as a glimmer of hope.

It's common to allow our engagements with people, places and things to separate us from the pursuit of the high aspirations we hold for ourselves. At the very least, they often tamper with our motivation and reasons for pursuing those dreams. For some, a relationship may run its course and result in a harsh separation or divorce. For others, getting fired from the job under the appearance of unfair circumstances sends them scampering in any direction that may stave-off financial collapse. Quite often, our default attitude is that these people, conditions and circumstances come along for the sole purpose of holding us back. They seem custom-designed to prevent us from following our hearts, pursuing our dreams and reaching our true potential. Feeling some great injustice has been leveled against us, we become angry, frustrated and resentful to the extent of becoming consumed by these emotions.

Unable to conquer the hurts and fears of the past, an attempt is made to "save face" and ward off the ghosts of guilt and abject failure by lowering our default expectations. With seemingly no choice, we surrender our "thrive" mentality to "survive" mode. Some do so by adopting a "do others before they can do me" hustler's mentality. Others simply opt for one of the multiple, elaborate "victim costumes" that are conducive for creating scams of incompetence and disability. The result of falling into this trap is that we fumble an opportunity to channel the energy of a deeply defining moment that points the way to our higher good. Stuck in a pattern of processing life experiences to our detriment, we squander opportunity after opportunity to cultivate the passion that is needed to propel us toward our dreams. Consequently, we shift our energy into non-productive channels that effectively block the flow of insight that would reconnect us with that which we have lost sight of: the path of our destiny and purpose.

For many, there is a much clearer vision of what they are inspired or directed by their hearts to do. Though passionate about their dreams, they, too, succumb to the pressures of popular opinion, the latest fad or a set of circumstances. As a result, they resentfully commit to paths that bring them little if any satisfaction. With very little of their heart invested, their only connection to their task is the proverbial "carrot at the end of the stick," better know as a paycheck and benefits. In pursuit of the carrot, we have converted the task of life achievement into a highly competitive, high-stakes, anything goes affair where the arts of sabotage, subterfuge and manipulation are highly coveted skills. As a result - while climbing the ladder of success - it is commonplace to encounter a host of angry, belligerent people, scratching and clawing their way along, in pursuit of whatever pacification lies at the top.

In seeking to understand the dynamics involved in establishing our unique kingdom, be clear that there are, without a doubt, occasions when persons enter our lives seeking to control our expression. They often come to mirror a direct reflection of our own often hidden senses of ineptness and timidity - i.e. to challenge our commitment to recovering the kingdom key. They show up as parents, relationship partners (past and present), children, employers, ministers, advisors, and anyone else whom we've placed in positions of influence in our lives. Often professing superior knowledge of what is best for us, they use guilt, threat, physical force, verbal persuasion, or any method thinkable to enforce their will and/or reinforce ours. Seeking to liberate ourselves from restraint and delay, we kick, scream, curse, and threaten all on our path in an effort to intimidate our way to a breakthrough. Meanwhile, "the one who knows," the one for whom this whole life drama is staged, sits at our center, patiently waiting for us to show up, align and get the necessary understanding.

Though we often use these and similar events as shovels to dig our own graves, their true nature is to bring us to crucial points for self-definition. They provide prime opportunities to go within for guidance that will enable us to see beyond the appearance to the "soul's intent."

The path from apprentice to journeyman is a deliberate one that requires intent, focus and practical application, as well as time. Rarely do we consider that the delay may be a timely one. It could be that we are not properly prepared to step into the opportunity we yearn for. The gifts, talents and skills required for the task may not have become fully developed. Your advancement may simply call for a little patience and a few more ticks of the clock. It could be that your commitment to self-determination requires more testing and tempering. Or could it be that an attitude adjustment is needed?

We often set ourselves up for mediocrity and mishandled opportunity through misinterpreting the truth behind the appearance of our experiences. Yet, you can believe that, as sure as we are living entities moving and creating on the Earth plane and beyond, there is a gathering process going on within our souls. Our lives are patterned on a grand design. It is the nature of that design to allow us to assign whatever value we will to the experiences we attract to our lives. That being so, be mindful of what meaning you decide to attach to your life experiences.

When the pressure associated with our challenges and presumed slights subsides, and we experience some measure of breakthrough, it's common that we do our bit to thank the Source, while doing a much more enthusiastic victory dance over the effigy of those persons and circumstances we feel worked against us. Reasoning that "what they intended for harm, God intended for good," rather than embracing the opportunity to see that "all things work together for the goodness of our souls," we devalue the part the "nurses" played. Know that the circumstances that enter your life never come to destroy any part of you that is essential to your development into a fully actualized human being. The level to which you are able to see this and benefit depends on your level of consciousness. Defined as "a sense of one's personal or collective identity based reality," consciousness is what I refer to as "your Kingdom."

> *"Fear not little flock; for it is your father's good pleasure to give you the kingdom."* - Luke 12:32

The interpretation of the Kingdom that I got from my religious experience imaged it as some elusive, far off, white-columned, high rent district reserved for those who somehow manage to wade through the myriad of interpretations on the will of God, find the right one, perform it to perfection, die, and show up to be ushered onto the golden streets thereof. Well, for many it's just that. As heirs to the Kingdom, we have been given the right to establish boundaries where we may. Many, in lieu of searching for the key to the authentic kingdom, have chosen to establish surrogate kingdoms in a far-away land outside themselves. All of this is acceptable. As spiritual beings, we are so powerful that our interpretations are indeed our valid reality.

> *"The Father's pleasure is to give to you the kingdom, and deep within your heart you'll find the key - to release unto the world the only power to mend the broken heart and make the captive free."*
>
> I Come -(A Song of Spiritual Renaissance) - Raja

As you may have guessed, I have a different take on the kingdom. After many years of enrollment in the aforementioned school of thought (the one with the golden streets/white columns etc.), born of sitting in counsel with my Spirit, I've come to a different understanding. Rather than the "after while it will all be over" stuff that I took in from the take out joints, I've come to see the kindgom as an irrevocable seed of Genius buried somewhere beneath our lifetimes of rationalized mediocrity. Its glowing aura clearly distinguishes it from the dim half-light of unrealized potential. Therefore, the Kingdom - in all its vast, unlimited glory - constitutes complete awareness of who you are as a spiritual being, and an awareness of what aspect of that being you've come to deploy in this current life. It signifies the most grand and all-encompassing ambition you hold for your life and all who touch it; along with the gifts, talents, skills, and creative resources to bring that vision into being. It is this Kingdom that it gives the Father - the Source of the "All-Knowing Genius within" - great pleasure to give or reveal to you.

Jesus said to his disciples, (Luke 22:29 King James Edition), "And I appoint unto you a Kingdom, as my Father hath appointed unto me." Realizing (quite clearly and at an early age) that he came with a mission, that he must be about his Father's business, he said to his disciples (and I humbly submit to you) that each of us, by mutual consent, has been appointed a Kingdom, a domain, a realm of service. With our cumulative talents, sharpened insights and bolstered determination, we came...fully prepared to engage the path to which we are called. The blueprint of this "non-generic Kingdom" is within each of us.

## The "Non Generic" Kingdom of God

To draw an analogy from the information age, the Kingdom is similar to having your own domain name and website. To illustrate this point, I will use my domain address which is: www.rajaiam.com. If you were to type http://www.rajaiam.com into your Internet browser, because this URL (universal resource locater) is unique in the whole world, you would get the website that sets forth my intention. At my "home page," you would find general information about my mission and principles. There would also be links to my services, my on-line product store, a page where you can listen to samples of my work, and pages with biographical information. Following these connections or links will lead you to deeper levels within my domain where more specific information can be obtained.

Following this analogy, my web address represents the location of the domain or "Kingdom of RAJAIAM." The key to the kingdom is my domain name, "rajaiam.com." The information at the site, i.e. the mission statement, products, services, skills, talents, and other resources of the parent company and subsidiaries represents the kingdom's assets, hierarchy, infrastructure, topography, landscape, and other qualities and attributes. As my self-image expands, through the development of additional products, services and information, so do my boundaries and domain or realm of influence. To inform the market of my new viability, it would be necessary to periodically "update" the information I put out concerning who I AM.

Such is the case with your spiritual kingdom. As with rajaiam.com, once your domain name is reserved, it is no longer available to anyone else. This provides you with your own unique place to "show up," guaranteeing that, while there may exist another entity that is almost identical, there is never one that is exactly the same. That is your legacy as a spiritual being engaging the human drama. While there are many persons whose talents mirror yours, there is only one you with your unique destiny to fulfill.

I am sure many of you, as I, have had the experience of being mistaken for or told that you look just like someone else. After assuring them that we are not that person, often their response is: "Well you sure do have a twin in the world." And while there may be those who look, act and think similarly to us (and who may even have the same birth date and similar ambitions), our consciousness, kingdom or domain is unique and non-repeatable throughout the whole world. Even identical twins are proven to have their own distinguishing characteristics, personalities and, certainly, their own destinies. Consequently, that which you came to master in the world (your individual Genius) is germane to you. And since your consciousness or ideas about who you are in the universal scheme of things is your domain or kingdom, whether your kingdom is authentic or surrogate depends upon whether you have discovered the true key.

As a vessel into which the energy of divine creativity flows, the platter upon which your gift is served can be as narrow and restrictive or broad, plentiful and all encompassing as you desire. Therefore, the information you make available to others can (by design or default) attract them to your kingdom or repel them from it. When a market assessment determines that you have focused on too narrow a market, and calls for adjustment, depending upon your commitment to growth and expansion, you can adjust or stay the course. In pursuit of the overall mission, you can charge your subsidiaries or offspring with becoming fully expressed, dynamic and self-sustaining, or you can choose the role of a tyrant - ruling with the iron fist of inflexible, limited perception. As the sole ruler of your unique and distinguished kingdom, the choices are yours.

As a frequent user of the Internet, I am fascinated by the prospect of sending an e-mail correspondence to someone on the other side of the world and having them receive it in a matter of seconds. The entrepreneurial side of me is also thrilled at the prospect of having an "online store" where I can make this book and my music available around the world. Of the many features that are attractive to those doing business on the Internet, the one I hear most often touted is anonymity, or the fact that no one has to know who you are. Often fearing that a potential consumer may not like what he or she sees of our race, sex or general appearance, many choose to depersonalize their web sites by revealing little to no personal information about themselves. While these may indeed be good marketing tactics and smart maneuvers for protecting the bottom line, be mindful of the message you're sending yourself concerning self-acceptance and your belief in the viability, worthiness and overall integrity of your kingdom.

> *"I come that you might have life; I come to put an end to strife; I come that you might be free to fulfill your destiny."*
>
> I Come (A Song of Spiritual Renaissance) - Raja

No one can fully disclose the intricate details of the kingdom to you but the "Father" - your inner guide. When we "show up" and ask for guidance, we truly come to understand that it is the Father's good pleasure to give us the kingdom. No one can receive the key for us. We must claim it for ourselves. The longer we wait, the more difficult it may be to find.

## *Chapter Summary*

- From beyond the veil of limited human perception, we (as spiritual beings) orchestrate the events surrounding how we show up to engage the paths that fulfill our life purpose.

- At the level of soul, each of us has a clear understanding of what will bring wholeness and contentment to our lives.

- The fact that we awaken each morning is testament that this reality continues to reside within us, seeking fulfillment.

- We often suffer the misconception that people and/or conditions are designed to prevent us from reaching our true potential.

- Know that the circumstances that enter our life never come to destroy any part of us that is essential to our development into a fully actualized human being.

- Delays are often both needful and timely, as they grant space and time to temper our determination, and make adjustments to our approach to our goals.

- Each of us, by mutual consent and design, has been granted a kingdom, domain or realm of service. Therefore, that which we came to master in the world (our unique Genius) is germane to us.

- The "Kingdom" is one's consciousness or personal and/or collective sense of identity. It constitutes our level of awareness of who we are as a spiritual being, as well as our awareness of the resources at our disposal.

## In Pursuit of the Kingdom

- This "non generic" kingdom is within you.
- As spiritual beings, we are so powerful that our interpretations or perceived reality creates and validates our experience.
- As a vessel into which the energy of divine creativity flows, we have the option of being as narrow and restrictive or broad and all-encompassing as we desire.
- When we "show up" and ask for guidance, we are ushered into the understanding that "it is the Father's good pleasure to give us the kingdom."
- No one can claim the kingdom for us. We must claim it for ourselves.

A Task: Take a moment to consider the nature and integrity of your kingdom. What type of vessel are you? Search your heart to discover if you have found the key.

# Chapter 4

*Being in Integrity*

"A Kingdom divided against itself cannot stand."

Luke 11:17

Due, in large part, to the frequency with which malfeasance and other improprieties occur within the arenas of politics, business and other social realms, we are continually afforded the occasion to access a great deal of dialogue lending to the principle of integrity. The intense level of rancor and division that typify the politically polarized nature of many ot these events provide an unprecedented opportunity to examine what integrity means, at deeper levels within our own psyche. When I speak of integrity, I'm not talking about a set of moral or ethical codes gleaned from collective consciousness, and imposed upon the masses by institutional dictate. In my mind, there are basic, immutable and generally accepted tenets of integrity such as honesty, fairness and mutual respect. Given these basics, the balance of what integrity means is as independent a value as are the individual requirements of our soul growth.

The standard definitions that come most near to what I see define integrity as: "The state of being unimpaired - soundness;" and "The quality or condition of being whole or undivided - completeness." By our own spiritual design, we are here on a mission. How well we do (i.e. how complete we become) depends on how much of what we do can be integrated by our soul into fulfilling our "life-purpose." Bear in mind that the soul is constantly assimilating the motivating energies behind our thoughts, emotional impulses, feelings, words, and deeds. It is literally creating our legacy on the fly. So integrity, for me, is a commitment to being unimpaired by ulterior motive, as we feed our soul the quality of experience needed to contribute to its quest for ultimate integration - or Godhood. Simply stated, it is the ultimate expression of being true to ones' "Self."

We all experience times when the reasons for things we do are not clear, even to us. It seems that, in spite of our best efforts, we find ourselves operating "out of character..." times when we have to ask ourselves, "Where did that come from?" or "Why in the world did I do that?" These events happen at different levels of our growth, but particularly during times when we refuse to exercise personal discipline, or when we decide to surrender to the larger wisdom of our spirit - two seemingly different ends of the spectrum. When operating from the non-disciplined level associated with "victim's consciousness," it is beyond our kin to take personal responsibility for the things that move us one way or the other. The tendency is to always look outside ourselves for the cause of our foibles, even though the source is obvious and internal.

Even after having surrendered one's will to inner guidance, events seem to unfold in ways that literally baffle the senses. It is then that, in order to connect with the motivation behind my actions, I have found it most beneficial to get centered in my heart. In examining these questionable situations by assessing whether I have been honest and fair (operating from good intent) or whether my intent was to be malicious or harmful, I avoid "flogging myself into an emotional coma." If I am clear that my motivations are honorable, and that the dilemma is motivated by unseen forces and events that I have to allow to play out, there is nothing more I can do. That being so, regardless of who prefers that I hold on and continue to embellish the drama, I let it go. If, through earnest contemplation, I see that, though it escaped my conscious awareness, my motivations were not honest, and that my actions were not in integrity, I make the necessary adjustments and move forward.

Whenever our level of integrity or integration is less than our best and highest, along with circumventing the opportunity to apply what we do in the moment to our soul's quest for Mastery, we also compromise, pollute and dilute the collective energy resident within our souls. In doing so, we condemn ourselves to a perpetual ride on the merry-go-round of mediocrity. Therefore, it's important to be clear and honest about our intent, and resolve any issues of internal conflict as speedily as possible. When we allow our ego to cause us to vacillate or remain torn between two opinions, we guarantee the short-circuiting of our creativity, and invite energies that foster the potential undermining of our kingdom.

A common human tendency (and certainly an early one of mine) is to be full of opinion and overview concerning other peoples lives. I learned the hard way that it's not for me to judge whether another person is in integrity. Holding on to a firm set of ideas about what was "right" versus "wrong," and what I would never do that others were doing, propelled me into a period when I had "stuff" (and lots of it) cropping up in my life unannounced, but certainly not uninvited.

One particular set of issues that whipped me to a point near death, involved the absence of my father, and the subsequent role my stepfather played in my life. My father and mother separated before she knew she was pregnant with me, so I grew up with very few opportunities to interact with him. She got together with my stepfather when I was about two, and the fifteen years I lived under his rule though profitable, were painful. I seemed to have been cast in the role of his personal whipping boy, and spent a memorable amount of time wondering why such a difficult fate had befallen me. While suffering the slights of my stepfather, I spent years longing for my father's and mother's reunion. Well, that never happened and, as a result, the formulative years of my life were spent immersed in the feeling of not belonging anywhere. Yet, in examining the roles, images and ways of both men, I gleaned from each of them what I considered "positive" characteristics, which I incorporated into my way of being in the world. I also observed things that I literally swore to never duplicate and guess what? In direct contradiction to the strength of my convictions, these undesirable circumstances showed up on my plate!

The judgments that I made, years earlier, had come home to roost; and my sense of integrity and self-worth underwent a grave and severe dissection. When change, in the form of divorce, came to visit my family structure, even though I knew my soul was calling me to release, let go and embrace greater truths concerning the structure of family, I kicked myself around pretty well. I was the guy who swore to never put his kids through the tough scenario I experienced as a child. Yet, at what can clearly be termed a "defining moment," I knew that to be in integrity with myself, I would have to be considered "out of integrity" in the eyes of others. Those "others" included my wife, the church, my children, friends, extended family and, to a great extent, society at large. My move from the point of servicing the long-held commitment to keeping things intact despite the cost, to a point of solitary peace and contentment with my decision and myself has been a long and difficult journey. It took years for me to release the foreboding and to develop a healthy disposition concerning the amount of upheaval that was occurring in my life. But, with the help of others who were also beating me up, I finally arrived at a point of self-reconciliation. I also came to realize the truth and power of (Matthew 7:1-2) which says:

> *"Judge not that ye be not judged. For with what judgment ye judge, ye shall be judged: and with what measure ye mete, it shall be measured to you again."*

Re-examining my life through this filter provided a broader perspective on why I attracted certain conditions into my life. As "kingdom expanding experiences," they sent a clear message about the costs involved with judging someone else's integrity. Through releasing the tendency to judge others lives through the "custom-colored prism" of my own life, these experiences provided insight that helped me to stave-off potential repeats of the same pitfalls. With their aid, I also learn to be motivated by the things I desire, rather than focusing on what I dislike.

It is an imperative of spiritual growth that we confront each of our judgments in the mirror of Cosmic Reflection. It is through this process that we choose our modem for future growth. We can choose the accelerated route, by developing compassion, understanding, and acceptance. Or, by virtue of our choice to develop a deeper bond with hatred and disease, we can proceed down the path of pain and drudgery. With your idea of integrity defined by your individual spirit, your actions may not align with expectations others have for you. The path to self-determination is truly the "road less traveled." So, it will take guts and perseverance to stake out and establish your own kingdom...to become your own person...to follow your own heart. Expect that when you begin to listen to your heart, you will incur the wrath of those who have previously pulled your strings. Know that this is simply a test of your resolve. No one else can know your heart, and no one else can know or walk your path. When we truly connect with and are led by the "Law of the Kingdom," we begin to operate at the level of "grace and truth"- a level of consciousness that not only fulfills the law, but supersedes it. Once you are sure that you have connected with your inner guidance, exercise due diligence in

# Being In Integrity

following through; for you are then guided by the "Law of the Soul" - the highest law governing human experience.

*Following the Law of Your Soul*

> *"I'm no longer naive about the things that I believe, my truth unfolds eternally. It doesn't matter about the challenges that starting new may bring, it all comes down to loving me."*
>
> — The Voices of Change - Raja

An inherent trait of a person who has obtained Mastery in any area of life is an insistence on taking his or her own counsel, or upon "dancing to the beat of his or her own drum." While possessing a mind that is "open to everything yet attached to nothing," a person on the path to Mastery must insist on being the final authority on what is correct for his or her life. I have spent the larger part of my life building confidence in my own insights and inner promptings. Even though I appeared the perfect picture of independence and self-assuredness, I was far too often (once or twice) prone to yielding to someone else's ideas about my destiny and life direction. So, I tried a few of them. "You are called to be a preacher," some said. "You should get back together with your wife, because once married, married for life," said others. Then there were those who chimed in with "Your destiny is to remodel and build houses. Forget about that writing and music business." Add to these voices the inner demons (the fear thoughts) that prophesied doom and otherwise deadly consequences for not obeying these prophets, and you can imagine that I have literally wrestled with the angel (as did the biblical Jacob) for my blessing of self-determination.

One of the most difficult challenges I've had in following the law of my soul came, in the early 80's, while I was a young associate minister in a Pentecostal church. I spent years holding onto and reinforcing a narrow perception of truth. I found myself saying things from the pulpit and in my interactions with people that my heart could no longer own. As committed as I was to "follow my calling," when inner conflict arose, it became clear that I must follow my heart, or lose my soul. In challenging the things I didn't agree with, I was soundly ostracized, as well as branded a "backslider," "infidel" and a "nae-re-do-well." I, ultimately, decided that I would take no more...that it was time to reclaim my God-given right to be self-identifying and self-determinate.

The effects of this parting of the ways reached deeply into the bonds of my marital relationship, and sparked division between my wife and me. When she, echoing the church leadership, insisted that I would never do well until "I came back to the church" and began attempts to manipulate and coerce me toward that end, it became clear that she and I were not going to make it. It was clear that I would have to do the most difficult thing I have done in my life. Literally fighting for survival, I struggled to "rewire my inner circuitry" and ward off the voices of doom; voices that said: "You will never amount to anything if you leave this church;" voices that said: "Your life is cursed for leaving God and your family," and "You are just like your father." Yet, I had to go.

Over the ensuing years, I fought my way through false accusations, false arrests, deep depression, the stigma and threats associated with the "deadbeat dad" label, and many other efforts to intimidate me into doing other than what my spirit-guided soul would have me do. Though I - like Jacob - have had my "hip knocked out of joint" on several occasions, my motivation (the burning desire of my heart) has never swayed from the development of my soul as well as the souls of those I sponsored.

Despite the costs, I have remained committed to discovering and aligning with my soul's unique and powerful sense of integrity. This quest has delivered me from the despair that results from living to be loyal to others at the expense of loyalty to myself. The psychological and emotional maturity I've gained has fostered the understanding that lack of loyalty to oneself ultimately engenders resentment, hypocrisy and mediocrity in our dealings with others. Through listening to my own spirit, I have come to understand that the nature of my soul is determined by the quality of the choices I make and my commitment to taking responsibility for those choices. My choice to surrender the mediocre in pursuit of life mastery has led to the discovery of that rich core of being that is my truth. Consequently, I accept myself as the unique, fully-expressed, creative, celebratory soul that I, in truth, know that I AM: The "Master Dishwasher" - replete with unimpeachable integrity.

## *Summary*

- The definition of integrity (as defined by the dictionary) that comes closest to my view, defines it as: "the quality or condition of being whole, undivided; completeness."

- My definition of integrity is: "A commitment to being unimpaired by ulterior motive, as we feed our soul the quality of experience that contributes to its ultimate integration; Godhood." (Following the Law of Your Soul)

- The soul is constantly assimilating the motivating energies (emotions) behind our thoughts, feelings, words and deeds.

- By our own spiritual design, we are here on a personal mission of growth and unfoldment.

- How complete we become depends upon how much of what we do can be seamlessly integrated into our life purpose.

- Focusing on the things we do not desire generates the energy for attracting them into our lives. Focus on those things you desire, and draw them into your life.

- Judge not that ye be not judged. Regardless of how someone else's life appears, you do not have the vantage point offered from having walked in their shoes.

- With similar experience come empathy compassion and understanding.

- When you are led by the "Law of Your Soul," you will operate at the level of "grace and truth," which not only fulfills the law, but supersedes it. It is the highest law governing human experience.

- The path to self-determination is truly the "road less traveled."

- A person on the path to life Mastery is "open to everything, yet attached to nothing."

- No one else can know your heart, and no one else can know your path.

- True integrity demands that you follow the law of your soul.

A Task: What is your definition of integrity? Has your pursuit of the "Law of Your Soul" caused you to adjust the parameters of your definition? If so, explain how?

# Chapter 5

## *Motivation*

*"I never thought there would be true happiness for me; so I settled for survival, made "getting by" my destiny. But, I've reconnected with my dreams, and as I spread my tender wings, like the butterfly I AM I fly away."*

- Fly Away - Raja

As unique individuals walking our own paths, we have our own motivations for doing the things we do. Quite often, we have at least two: the one we tell ourselves and others, and the one that truly lies beneath it all, unrevealed - often times - to our own conscious minds. Take for instance the man who shows up daily on a job he despises, puts in his eight hours and, as a matter of routine, heads to the liquor store en route home. Upon his arrival, he grunts a response to greeting from his family, retires to the den with his best friend the TV remote, drinks himself to sleep, and awakens in the morning to start the routine over. Projecting and professing a state of discontent, when the inner voice of his conscious asks what has motivated him to maintain this life of drudgery, he takes another drink and responds: "I'm just doin' what I gotta do to survive man."

Consider the woman who is in a relationship that has proven dangerous for her emotional and physical health, yet she stays. After another tumultuous, fear-ridden night of verbal and physical abuse, though grief stricken, she awakens to prepare for work. Having witnessed her children trembling in stark terror the night before, she can spend but a moment consoling them with a song, as they prepare for school. With all sick leave and vacation time exhausted from numerous call-ins, resulting from injurious conflict, her body and psyche wounded and her job on the line, the Lord of the Kingdom beckons her to counsel seeking her motivation for drinking ceaselessly from the bitter cup of self-deprecation. Out of her broken spirit and wounded soul, she confides that it is her desire to do more to utilize her gift for singing that sets the stage for this ongoing persecution. She states that, even though her yearning will not cease, her love for her man is too strong for her to break the shackles, and rise above her current circumstance. She confides that rather than be alone, she would harness her divine creativity and endure an occasional affront to her self-worth and well-being, while seeking to quiet the voice of destiny.

Let's visit with a dedicated church member who, for years, has felt the need to grow beyond the confines of restrictive religious indoctrination. Service after service, year after year, he or she sits and quietly ingests things that are familiar and, yet, disagree with his or her inner truth. Rationalizing an inability to do without church fellowship, yet gossiping about their discontent to others, the Lord of the soul stands at the door and knocks, saying: "If anyone will open unto me, my Father and I will come in and sup with him (or her), and make our abode." Ignoring the knock, the choice is made to opt for joining the choir, in hope that the harmonious blending of voices will override the incessant droning that resonates from a disconsolate soul.

## *Life's Four Basic Motivators*

To some extent, I have lived each of these lives - playing one role or the other. Thus, I can say with certainty that fear, in one form or another, lies at the root of most of our reasons for not moving forward to make positive adjustments in our lives. It's abundantly clear that, by default, our social indoctrination programs us for lives of hapless co-dependency. For instance, the "what would I do without you" theme of most popular music is a testament to our lack of a healthy sense of our independent value and potential. The fear of lowering our approval rating, in the eyes of others, and, thereby, losing their acknowledgment and support; the fear of change and the uncertainty and instability that it often brings; and the fear of having to walk our path alone, unaccompanied by a "significant other" have been responsible for sending masses into the graves of apathy and resignation.

The desires for companionship, camaraderie and connectivity are the natural urges of the soul seeking union and wholeness. Yet, our penchant for dimming our own inner light to "pilot light status" in order to manipulate others into remaining in relationship engenders an unhealthy co-dependency that sickens the soul. This motivation to manipulate others to get what we want is not limited to intimate relationships, but encompasses the entire realm of human endeavor.

While motivations come under many guises and with a variety of window dressing, I feel that there is a set of four basic areas of motivation. These four encompass the entire realm of human endeavor:

(1) That which we do to obtain money, status and power.

(2) That which we do for acceptance and approval.

(3) That which we do out of habit.

(4) That which is born of passion.

It is a simple and easily verifiable fact that where so called "positive pursuits" are concerned, most people never get past the first three reasons to the point where passion is the primary drive for their positive efforts. With a large amount of the motivational material we see today supported by the nebulous energy of such catchy phrases as "Just Do It!" (the popular Nike commercial phrase), the emphasis is on performing whether we feel connected to the act or not, or on "profiling" and looking good for the cameras while we are "just doing it." Then there is how much we're getting paid for doing it, and how others are responding to what we are "just doing." We give little thought to connecting with our source to examine our motivation to determine whether what we are "just doing" is doing our souls any good.

Operating in an unconscious mode, in pursuit of short-term gratification, we muddle around, expend a great deal of energy and experience a series of moderate successes and near misses, while never becoming "in love" with what we are doing or with whom we are doing it. That includes ourselves. This way of being has been enforced and reinforced in the minds of many by the apparent success of many high-profiled con artists. These include some rap artists and athletes who, by their own admission, have no real connection to what they are rapping about or love for the game they are playing. They admit to just "getting paid," not realizing that the benefits (while lavish and ego gratifying) are short-term and of little substance to the soul. It is the good fortune of some to ultimately realize that the true payoff is a loss of integrity with Self. Those who make the adjustment to connect with the law of their soul, to discover its intent, and become fueled by its passion are blessed to discover life's truest and greatest rewards.

It's evident that we live in a society where our value is assigned on a basis of how high-profile and/or well paid we are. In essence, our "net worth" and "self worth" are often viewed by us and others as interchangeable. This is our truth and our legacy, to date. This is the way we have chosen to have it, and there are many valid arguments for keeping it this way. Yet, in the newly emerging paradigm of the twenty-first century, it will become incumbent upon us to consider all things in the context of their overall contribution and value to the type of society we desire to form.

In choosing our fields of expertise, it has been our habit to select those we felt would give us the best opportunity for remaining viable and competitive for the long haul, rather than those that really spoke to us and lit a fire inside. In speaking of those things we loved to those whose opinions we respected, the reception we received was often just pointed enough to dampen our spirits and send us in an alternative direction. Engaged in the pursuit of status and security, yet lacking the conscious awareness that "our kingdom is not of this world," we set out to establish kingdoms of brick, mortar, wood, metal, paper, and stone. We adorn these kingdoms with recognized symbols of success (the material things that seem to say we've "made it") yet, in the deepest recesses of our souls, we face the question "Is this all that you desire of the kingdom?" We are reminded to Seek first the kingdom of God and its righteousness (or right thinking), and all of these things will be added unto us.

A prime example of an inordinate sense of motivation and value is evidenced in what we, as a society, are willing to pay athletes versus, say, teachers. I am a sports enthusiast who revels in the mastery of athleticism and sportsmanship displayed on the field, hardwood, links, court, or wherever a ball is bouncing. As an entrepreneur, I clearly understand the thrust of the free enterprise system, in which I willingly participate. Yet, I can't help but question whether we suffer some strange psychosis that prevents us from seeing how (through our inordinate value system) we are plotting our own demise. We have complained, for years, that American children lag far behind children of other nations in terms of educational prowess and certain critical skill levels. We knew that this dilemma would ultimately translate into a diminished pool of qualified workers to service a rapidly growing, technology-driven job market. Yet, at very basic levels, it's clear that our commitments to primary and secondary education and those who serve that domain are pathetic.

Our societal priorities are such that we pay hundreds of thousands of dollars per game to athletes whose primary contribution to society is the consistency of their jump shot or ability to hit a baseball three times out of ten. Conversely, we pay twenty five to thirty-thousand dollars per year to the teacher to whom we shift a great deal of the responsibility for preparing our children for the world. It's an easy thing to say that one has nothing to do with the other, that one scenario underscores the beauty of free enterprise while the other exposes the inequities that occur when institutions are overly regulated by government. The fact is that it is our responsibility, as a society and human community, to establish standards that reflect our best and highest aims. Fact is, as unseemly as it appears, that's exactly what we are doing.

A balanced and enlightened society demands equitable consideration for those who contribute to the uplifting of the society. Yet, as long as the economy continues to "blow up," and our fairytale kingdoms are not affected, its an easier task to "pass the beer, click the remote, and let the good times roll." Unwilling to upset the apple cart, little to no thought is given to how we are narrowing our path and cultivating a difficult row for our children and future generations to hoe. Undermining the educational system, through maintaining archaic models for both instruction and compensation, precludes an easily predictable outcome of cultural and financial demise.

The allure of status and worldly power has historically extracted a large toll from those who have become intoxicated from drinking too deeply from its well. Yet, the desire for power, money, and status plays out at lower levels of the financial spectrum, as well. A daily concern with issues of financial security and basic survival cause us to remain connected to jobs, relationships, and other commitments that have served their purpose for our lives. In that we've become attached to their contribution to our ability to pay the bills and maintain our "good standing," we acquiesce, knowing that no meaningful soul enhancement is being provided to our lives. Fearing the loss of creditability and, thereby, integrity, we choose to hold on and maintain the status-quo. Resigning to "fight the good fight" and "do the right thing;" we choose to defer our dreams and our happiness until our elusive "change comes." Failing to comprehend that the most positive and beneficial advancement is that which is self-initiated, we remain gripped by fear and mired in mediocrity.

It is a given that the leap from where we are to where we desire to be is an often difficult and even frightful step. It may require that we leap empty handed across an open abyss. I would be less than honest in saying that the pivotal changes I've made in life were anything that resembled a breeze. But I've lived enough life in the shadows of someone else's truth about my potential to know that my only salvation was in making that leap. I am clear that my principle area of mastery involves the art of sharing my life experiences and the understandings I've gleaned from them in written, spoken and musical forms. The struggle I had in moving from doing what was paying the bills (home improvement) to what which my heart longed to do required that I (for a time) do both. Embracing the fact that I would experience many challenges, such as the clear prospect of non-instantaneous financial gratification (being broke), I made the commitment to engage my path and take it all the way. In spite of my encounter with severely challenging times, I have never entertained the idea of turning back. In fact, since I am simply being who I am and doing what I do, there is no back!

I have intimate knowledge of the challenges of not having sufficient money to meet my basic responsibilities. That isn't easy! I know how tough it is to stay positively motivated and passionate when you arise daily to go to a job that, after paying the bills, provides barely enough enough to get you there and back. I know how difficult it is to keep the channels clear and maintain an attitude of positive expectancy when, for years, following your dream has taken all the faith and resources you could muster and there is no breakthrough in sight. Yet, that's exactly what you've got to do.

At several points along the journey, I became quite agitated at having to struggle so hard to take care of the necessities while creating a space for manifesting my heart's desire. I had a deep and burning desire to make the leap into doing what I yearned to do, and have it afford the life I desire to live. In the midst of these emotionally challenging times, my ability to hear from within that I was on the right track subverted the potential for frustration and resentment. A little introspection revealed that mine was a battle with issues involving old, deeply-embedded personal image paradigms, or old ideas that were challenging my newly emerging senses of integrity and responsibility. It seems that I needed to clearly commit to not vacillate between two opinions on my definitions of integrity and responsibility - to decide that it was really "OK" for me to take the risk to follow my heart. Though I knew I would face some tough times, to take the risk and follow my heart was and remains my choice. I mounted the starting blocks, and with the "kingdom key" firmly in hand, I did my little "ready, set, go," and took off running. While facing many tough challenges, including the appearance of financial peril and just plain lack, my soul continues to feast on the passion that is generated from doing that which I know is right and perfect for me.

Through false starts, disappointment, fear, and discouragement, and with the bill collectors hounding you daily, you've got to find a way to establish and maintain control of your emotional and psychological energies. You've got to find a way to make your challenges work for you and not against you. You've got to think the right thoughts and, thereby, generate the right feelings or you will murder your hope and undermine your chances for advancing your affairs.

*A Willingness to "Buck Tradition"*

I have a friend, a wonderful brother who has found his passion. Peter Moore, a gifted musician and producer, has made a major contribution to my musical works. I have a tremendous appreciation for his awesome talent, and I highly recommend his abilities to anyone at any level of the music industry. Yet, beyond that, I am clearly aware of his "Spiritual Self" as the producer of the musical works he manifests. As I clearly receive the benefit of inner guidance in choosing to utilize certain words, Peter hears "the voice" in his selection of instruments, rhythm patterns and musical phrasing. In a conversation some time ago, he related his experience of arriving at the point of deciding whether to continue along a path that was expected of him or to follow his heart.

After graduating high school, Peter attended college with the intent of becoming a medical doctor - a precedent established by his father, two brothers and a sister. After receiving an undergraduate degree in Biology and acceptance into Drexel University to pursue a Master's in

Biomedical Engineering, Peter received a message from the Lord of the Kingdom to come sit in counsel. Upon examining his heart, he emerged assured that the nature of his kingdom was unique and different from those established by his father and siblings. Peter now faced the unenviable yet invigorating task of communicating his new direction to his family. You can only imagine the feedback he received. Yet, having established the realm of music as his domain, Peter enrolled at the University of Michigan, at Flint, where he obtained a degree in Music History and Theory.

Needless to say, Peter's announcement did not fly well with his family. It's not easy or comfortable to release old patterns and expectations, or to buck tradition and step onto a path we feel compelled to follow. Yet, if you ever make contact with the flame of your innermost desire - as did Peter and as have I - if you ever get your hand on the key, you will be so turned on and truly motivated that you will not stop your pursuit until you have taken full possession of your kingdom. As I work closely with Peter, I can attest to the fact that his passion for creating music is clearly evident in the compositions he produces. It is also clear to me that his Genius is revealed, his Mastery is apparent and greatness is his destiny.

What is the motivation behind the things you do? What is it that turns you on? What stirs a fire so deep down-inside your heart that if commanded by angels to give it up, you would adamantly refuse? What is it that would cause you to endure the ridicule of family, friends and associates and start all over at the level of dishwasher if that is what is required to keep the fire burning? Can it be found within the limited confines of the pursuit of fame and fortune? Is it fulfilled in the pursuit of financial ends without regard for making a valuable, in-kind contribution to life? Is its fullness found in relationship with another individual with whom you cannot do without? Or is it the creative energy that motivates you to delve deeper into your soul to discover greater possibilities for self-definition and expression? If it exists, if you've identified it, examine its authenticity. Be passionate about it. Make your calling and election sure, because that very thing constitutes the foundation of your kingdom. It is the link between you, the God of your soul and all of the resources and assistance required to bring your ideal into manifestation.

Without passion and true connectedness (which can only be obtained by embarking the path that leads to alignment with our purpose), what we do - while making a default and nominal contribution to the building of our souls - never propels us in the direction of life mastery. It is, at best, another monument in our ongoing tribute to mediocrity and a lack of integrity with Self. This lack of integrity (integration) with the spiritual part of one's being or one's "True Self" fosters a sense of disconnection that strips us of the ability to gain the greater rewards derived from considering all that we do as Godly service. When we are in alignment with the truth of our existence, we understand and accept that Mastery, in any area, requires the purest and most basic of motivations, one so clearly exemplified by the great educator Marva Collins and exemplary athlete Michael Jordan: that we do a thing - first and foremost - because we love it.

## *Summary*

- The four basic areas of motivation that generally encompass the realm of human endeavor are:

    (a) That which we do to obtain money, status and power.

    (b) That which we do for acceptance and approval.

    (c) That which we do out of habit.

    (d) That which is born of passion.

- When it comes to so called "positive" pursuits, most people never reach the point where passion is the primary sustainer of their efforts.

- Motivated by catchy phrases such as "Just Do It," we, quite often, give little thought to connecting with our inner guidance to determine whether what we are "just doing" is doing us any good.

- It is rare to find those who are "in love" with what they are doing or with whom they are doing it - including themselves.

- Operating unconsciously, with "getting paid" as one's primary motivation, results in short-term benefits. The real payoff is an ultimate loss of integrity with self.
- We live in a society where our "net worth" and "self-worth" are often viewed as synonymous and interchangeable.
- In pursuit of status and security, yet lacking conscious awareness that our kingdom is not of this world, we settle for kingdoms built of brick, mortar, wood "paper," and stone.
- Passion and true connectedness naturally propel us in the direction of true Mastery and fulfillment.
- Mastery, in any area, requires the purest and most basic of motivations: That we do a thing, first and foremost, because we love it.
- What do you love? "Seek first the Kingdom of God and its righteousness (right thinking), and all of these things will be added unto you."

Motivation

A Task: Take a moment to examine your motivations. List those things or the single thing about which you are most passionate. Ask yourself, "If I built upon this thing, would it provide a solid enough foundation to "support my kingdom" or fuel my life with a sense of purpose and fulfillment?

# Chapter 6

## *The Anatomy of A-TASK*

*"Whatsoever thy hand findeth to do, do it with thy might."*

Ecclesiastes 9:10

Earlier, I mentioned the struggle I engaged during the last year or so of the approximate 15 years I did home improvement. There were other times when my work had really become a chore, but never like this. Despite the struggle, I am particularly proud to say that the quality of the work I produced never suffered. Long ago, I made a commitment to myself to always do the best job of which I was capable at whatever I attempted. In spite of the drag I felt when I thought about the rut I imagined I was in, a wonderful quality of connectedness and release came over me as soon as I showed up and began working. As a result, I was always able to lend myself fully to the job at hand. This work ethic is a quality that I observed in my stepfather, father and mother, and incorporated into my life. They each had the kind of focus and commitment that compelled them to do what was before them without delay, and with a consistently high level of self-expectancy. They modeled that expectation for me and everyone with whom they interacted. You just didn't do a shoddy job around either of them and get away with it.

As a child, I often observed my stepfather's methods while building and repairing things around the house. He was a person who could do anything. I recall standing at the window watching as he lie on his back beneath his car, replacing the starter, in the dead-cold of a snowy, Northeastern Ohio winter. With a deep sense of appreciation for who he was, I vowed to be just as committed to the things I did. His example inspired me to never allow perceived obstacles and limitations to stop me from accomplishing either mundane tasks or my dreams.

## The Tao of Dishwashing

I can't forget the many years my mother worked two jobs. She retired, in 1995, after over 30 years of cleaning schools for the Barberton City School System. Her second job involved similar tasks at a dry cleaners, (Voris Cleaners) where she often took me along to help scrub and wax floors. She was a great teacher and a strict supervisor. I recall how, in her wonderfully adamant way, she would insist, often with a thump on the head, that I did the job right or I should get out of the way so that she could do it herself. I can hear her now saying: "Stop half-assing! Give me that mop and get out of the way." For some, this would have been a welcome reprieve, but for me, though in the early years of my pursuit of Mastery, this was tantamount to a kick in the shins. You see, I really wanted to learn how to do it right. So, momma was there to make sure I committed to putting my whole ass into it.

While working toward closure in the realm of remodeling, it became evident that my spirit was guiding me through several interesting and important lessons. There were qualities within my soul that needed strengthening, and remodeling continued to serve as the proving ground for whether I had properly assimilated them. To some extent, there were latent tendencies that needed purging from my consciousness. One lesson centered on the way I viewed the things I was doing in the present as they relate to the things I desire to do - i.e., the value and significance I gave them. I was truly proud that through my experiences, I had grown from a young man with a delicate self-image about what I could accomplish to someone who could do practically anything. It was my way, even then, to not discard the skills and knowledge accrued from past experiences, but to bring them forward to utilize or hold in reserve for potential, future use. Therefore, I clearly saw the practical and psychological value that learning to build things held for me and how I could transfer that knowledge into building my life vision. Yet, the simple fact is that I had come to view home improvement as something I couldn't wait to get away from. And though I found myself fully given to the task once engaged, the fact is that I had come to consider the whole process a burden.

Relieving my agitation required that I make peace with home improvement. Simply stated, the lesson is that of valuing and honoring that which you are doing in the present in the same fashion you would value and honor that which you desire to do - or that which you view as your dream job or career. In reality they are one and the same. Since the only time we can show up is "in the moment," the way we choose to be toward what we are doing in the moment is the barometer with which our souls assess our disposition or attitude and effort. These are the resources that provide the fuel for advancing our state in life. Be mindful that "all things work 'together' for the goodness of our souls."

When you build a commitment within your soul to connect with and honor all things (to be in integrity with them), you engender rich spiritual experience, and pave the way for future success. This is the path of the apprentice seeking journeyman status. In pursuit of mastery, he embraces the minute aspects of apprenticeship for whatever bits of value they bring to his process. Chief among these benefits are discipline and the practical application of the routine principles of his craft. He understands that a firm grasp of and commitment to the application of the fundamentals will gain the attention of the Master Journeyman and, consequently, afford him precious time under his watchful eye and tutelage.

*Passion Deferred*

How often have we deluded ourselves into thinking that when our "dream situation" comes along, we will, then, be able to surrender our whole hearts, generate unlimited reserves of passion and, thereby, forge our success? How many times have we changed jobs, lovers, houses, cars, churches, and cities under the guise of personal regeneration? How many times did we discover that, after a short while, the old us has resurfaced with a new dilemma and a new set of rationalizations? The fact is there are no reserves of passion to call upon if you haven't generated them and stored them in your soul. The way to do this is to connect with each and everything you do at a level of integrity and respect that will generate the quality of passion required to manifest your desires. To do so requires that you place your motivations under the tutelage of the impulse for mastery, resident within your soul. The King James Bible states it this way, in Ecclesiastes 9:10:

> *"Whatsoever thy hand findeth to do, do it with thy might; for there is no work, nor device, nor knowledge, nor wisdom, in the grave where thou goest."*

Here is what I see in this scripture: The soul is constantly assimilating the qualitative energy that we emit with each thought, feeling, word, and action. The importance, therefore, of doing with all your might whatever your hands find to do lies in these facts: 1 - There is no valid contribution to your soul's quest for Mastery, (no work) 2 - There is no applied principle or pattern of consistency (no device); 3 - There is no connection to and appreciation for the present and, therefore, no ability to transfer the benefits of what you are now doing (no knowledge); 4 - There is no self-empowering concept of why things are not working out or coming together (no wisdom); in the grave where thou goest; or in the mindset of dispassionate disconnectedness and indifference...a place we go far too often to do much of what we do.

## "A Task" Defined

As I stated in the introduction, the soul is as engaged during the seeming insignificant moments (or during the small and often mundane tasks) as it is when we are enjoying ourselves the most. So when we say "My heart just isn't in it," how mistaken we are. While it is often true that we disengage the guidance that would naturally flow from our Spirit, the fact remains that our soul is at the center of all we do. So, while you declare that your heart isn't in it, your soul always is. My decision to embrace and make peace with my remodeling tasks paved an integral stretch of the road leading to the front gate of my kingdom. These skills provided the foundation and the majority of the funding for the completion of my "Voices of Change" and "God Thang" music CD's. It also provided space for heeding the call to write this book.

At the time of this writing, I am participating in the fulfillment of a dream of Peter's, by putting the final touches on a studio that I built in the basement of his home. The trade-off is wonderful, as we each pour excellence, mastery and a love for what we do into these processes. My ability and willingness to do this work and the spirit with which I do it have afforded me the services of a top-notch producer/musician and friend, as well as the services of a cadre of his gifted and wonderfully spirited acquaintances.

If you have no fire or passion burning at the core of everything you do, you owe it to yourself and to that thing to either change the way you are viewing and interacting with it or to leave it alone. Get away from it! Just "Don't do it!" Your soul is saying: "I would that you were either cold or hot." Your choice to be lukewarm will cause your efforts to be rejected as having no value to your soul's quest for Mastery. If your decision is to change the way you interact with a condition, while you generate passion around it and allow it to work for your good, you will be required to exercise a bit of discipline over your thoughts and emotions. This will require that you incorporate a new pattern of enthusiasm into your thought processes. In order to do so, you may have to employ a little bit of psychology. Understanding that my soul requires a certain quality of integration to fuel its efforts toward Mastery, in assessing the way I spend my energy, I decided to refer to my efforts as "tasks" rather than chores or jobs. In a practical way this is somewhat like building a fire to fuel my efforts.

When we were children, we were often called upon to gather small sticks of wood that the elders called kindlin.' These small, almost splinter-like pieces of wood were used to get the fire started and to ignite the larger pieces. Technically, the process is called kindling a fire. In order to gain the greater benefits from our efforts, a similar psychological process is often necessary to stimulate our mental and emotional natures. When doing what may seem mundane tasks, to help shift my consciousness to more productive levels, I came up with an idea that I call "The Anatomy of A-TASK." I consider A-TASK to be - "Activity Toward Arousing Spiritual Kindling," or fuel for the fire needed to burn away the shackles that keep us bound to the merry-go-round of mediocrity. By viewing each task as a contribution to the building of my soul or character, I make a conscious decision to do my best in all things - at all times. In doing so, I've discovered a wonderful truth: The key to awakening the sleeping Genius within our soul is to offer to feed it passion, and to follow through in everything we do.

## *Summary*

- Our resistance to or frustration with an experience will, quite often, bind us to it. The surest way to get beyond it and avoid having to encounter it again on similar terms is to embrace or make peace with it.

- The quality of our interaction with the people, conditions and circumstances of our lives is the barometer by which our soul generates energy for creating new conditions and opportunities in our lives.

- By being in integrity with all that enters our lives, we engender rich spiritual experience, and pave the way for future success.

- We often delude ourselves into thinking that a change of cities, jobs, mates, residences or churches will revive our passion, and set us, squarely, on the path to happiness. This approach does little more than send us on an endless outer pursuit of that which can only be found within.

- The passion that we think we would have for our "dream job," "dream mate," "dream home," etc. will eventually die out, if our penchant for being passionate is not what drew the experience to us.

- If we are to obtain Mastery, passion must be generated within, stored within, and liberally applied to all of our endeavors.

- A-TASK is: "activity toward arousing spiritual kindling."

- It is the desire of your soul that you be cold or hot; therefore, whatever your hands find to do, do it with thy might."

- The key to awakening the sleeping Genius within your soul is to offer to feed it passion, and to follow through in everything you do.

## The Anatomy of A-TASK

A Task: What are some of the attitudes you have about the job you currently do, the relationship you are in, or any other condition that might be undermining your pursuit of greater opportunities? What adjustments do you feel would be to your benefit?

*Chapter 7*

## The Analogy of Dishwashing

*"But in a great house there are not only vessels of gold and of silver, but also of wood and of earth; and some to honor and some to dishonor."*

- II Timothy 2:20

In receiving the title, "The Tao of Dishwashing," it was immediately clear that the task of dishwashing contains both metaphoric and actual implications for the ideas I would share. The principle of honoring the least of things and doing the most basic of tasks with an attitude of appreciation and commitment to excellence applies to dishwashing, as well. In the literal sense, the job of dishwasher and/or busboy is the most entry of entry level jobs in the restaurant business. Along with such jobs as sanitation engineer, janitor and fast food restaurant employee, it conjures, for some, the image of a job that is low-end, mediocre and insignificant. For some, this makes these tasks unworthy of much respect or, maybe, our best effort. As for me, I am quite grateful for the conscientious garbage collector, short order cook and those who clean rest rooms and perform what might be considered menial tasks. My respect for them is no less than what I have for a governor who governs well or a musician, architect or athlete who pours love and passion into his or her craft. The fact is that each of these jobs, as well as the job you are doing at this point along your journey, is a potential springboard for Life-Mastery. The distance you are advanced along the path depends upon the level of character, dedication and integrity you bring to the job.

The task of dishwashing has historically garnered a great deal of resistance. In fact, if not for the invention of the automatic dishwasher, it would remain the most dreaded among household tasks. I recall that in our family of eight children, someone was forever attempting to trade off his or her dishwashing assignment. Cringing at the thought of scrubbing those burnt spaghetti pots and macaroni dishes, we were willing to trade chores, assist with homework and throw in a little change or whatever we could barter, within reason, to get someone else to do our dishes. I've observed the same pattern with my children. It seems that dishwashing never has been nor does it appear destined to become the craze or "the bomb."

Personally, I love dishwashing, and have come to value it as a significant endeavor from which I have received great benefit. I experience a contagious, soothing quality while washing dishes and have conveyed this discovery to several of my friends. Their response was to invite me over after dinner to wash their dishes...an invitation I obviously declined. I must confess that I didn't always enjoy this task. But through disciplining myself to connect with it and do it well, I've gained practical and spiritual insights into the path of self-mastery. As with any other task, I establish and enter into a zone that has produced quite a few creative ideas that I have incorporated into my song writing. As you read on, you will discover that the intricate details of the hand dishwashing process are utilized to underscore the principles I share.

In the most basic sense, I honor dishwashing because when I reach for a glass, plate, cup, knife, fork, or any cooking utensil (for my use or to serve others), and discover that it is not clean, I am not pleased. If you discovered some food particle glued to the rim of a glass from which I offered you drink, it could not only prove embarrassing, but could also contaminate, pollute or make less than pure that which I intended for your enjoyment. The same is true if I am served from items that are not clean. I also honor dishwashing because, within the various stages of its process, I discovered distinct parallels for the process of purging the soul of any residue of mediocrity or that lukewarm agent that prevents us from doing our best and becoming vessels to honor.

As I began the serious search for my life purpose, I realized it would be necessary for me to "clean up my act," so to speak. So, I began to inspect my consciousness to ferret out those potentially undermining spots and blemishes that had, heretofore, limited me to walking in the mere shadows of my true self. It's not that I was living in a state of rebellion against the will of Spirit, or living in a way that flew into the face of my own sense of integrity. In fact, it was quite the opposite. I had arrived

# The Analogy of Dishwashing

at a point where there was nothing more important than connecting with my true purpose and sharing my gifts in ways that would both satisfy my soul and benefit the world. I knew that in order for this to happen, my soul (the dish or vessel into which this Mastery would be poured) would have to be inspected and fortified. So, I made a conscious choice to engage a process for purging it of any potentially contaminating energy. So, in my spirit, I heard, and I say to you: "Examine: who you are, how you show up in the world, your commitment to being in integrity, the motivation behind your ambitions, and how you approach the things you do. And, as you are willing and as there is need, allow me to teach you the 'Tao of Dishwashing.'"

## *Summary*

- Every task, job or expenditure of energy should be considered significant.
- The job you are currently doing has within it lessons or opportunities that provide a springboard to Life-Mastery.
- The distance you are advanced along the path depends upon the level of character, dedication and integrity you bring to the task.

A Task: Take an honest inventory of the jobs or tasks that you feel you could not or would not do. How do you feel about the people who do these jobs? Do you honor them for their ability to handle tasks that you could or would not; or do you hold them in disdain, feeling that they do these tasks because they have no other choice? Can you, from the perspective of non-judgmental observation, recall anything within your life experience that has fostered these perspectives?

# Chapter 8

*Assessing the Washing Environment: Your Spiritual Practice*

*"In my father's house are many mansions: if it were not so I would have told you. I go to prepare a place for you."*

-St. John 14:

As I mentioned earlier, dishwashing is my metaphor for purging the soul to prepare for the unfolding of Mastery in your life. This is the point at which we delve into the particulars of this step-by-step process. To determine whether you are properly equipped for the task, the first step involves examining the environment and tools you utilize. This includes assessing everything from your sink to how and where you store the dishes upon completion. Your sink is synonymous with the place (physical and/or metaphorical) where you pull aside to commune with inner guidance. Whether a matter of regular worship service that is inclusive of others, or the private practice of sitting in the stillness, walking, running, quietly listening to music, reading a book, or entering into a deliberate meditation, the environment or "mansion" must suit your preference. What is important is that it is a place you are committed to going to get some "inner work" done, rather than a place you go to hide out.

It may be your preference to engage an organized form of religion; be it Christianity, Buddhism, Islam, Taoism, Hinduism, Judaism, or any of the other more than eleven thousand religions currently in existence. If so, in that there is a foundational element of universal truth resting at the core of all religion, the denomination does not matter. If you can avoid the politics, and navigate your way through the fog of rules, regulations and requirements to get to that core, religion can provide the spark that ignites your desire for the God flame. Be clear that the mere fact that you show up and engage the ritual is not enough to insure the results required to engage the Master Dishwasher. In fact, organized religion is one of the most expedient hiding places for those who lack the courage and discipline to "work out their own soul's salvation." I would also be careful of those places that claim to be the "only way" and the "only place" where the truth of God can be found. Your engagement with the Master Dishwasher will, ultimately, avail you to the truth that the creative source of all that is (that welcoming embrace that we call God) is everywhere and present in everything.

Research has shown that a greater level of bacteria exists in the area of the average kitchen sink than in and around the bathroom commode. Therefore, it's imperative to take the necessary steps to sanitize our environment. As our quest for spiritual understanding broadens, so do the efforts of those latent energies that have historically feasted upon our penchant for being weak-minded, lax and easily led. In choosing your environment, make sure you are not establishing your work station in an area that is infested with philosophical bacteria that may prove needlessly upsetting to your digestive system. Learn to listen to your own inner voice and seek out those spaces and experiences that speak to your spiritual desire. If something is not working for you, though it may have proved to be perfect in the past, leave it alone and move on to something else. Refuse to succumb to a religious environment or practice that fulfills someone else's desire for you, yet fails to serve the needs of your soul. The act of attending church because someone else feels you should is an affront to the development of a connection with your own spiritual voice.

In my experience, I have found it necessary to make many adjustments in my washing environment. As a youngster of twelve or thirteen years old, in Barberton Ohio, I was very active in a Pentecostal church. As the daughter of a Pentecostal minister in Pennsylvania, my mother had her fill of church, early on. And, except for Easter, she never required that we attend. So, I did so of my own volition. Although the preacher's four daughters became an immediate extra attraction, my initial interest was singing; so I joined for the chance to sing in the choir. Even at this age, I had a great enthusiasm for church. In fact, whenever I got on my folk's "bad side," my punishment was that I could not go to church. Though I don't think this would work well on many children today, it not only seemed cruel and unusual punishment, but leveled a devastating blow to my pursuit of truth. With the exception of a couple of years spent sowing a few "worldly oats," I remained dedicated to this practice late

## Your Spiritual Practice

into my twenties. After years of attending an average of five services a week, and contorting my consciousness and soul to conform to church doctrine, it became crystal clear that a change was due. Spurred on by a round of disruptive events, I began my solitary search for "true spirituality." Though I admit to having felt out of sorts in the early stages of my shift, through learning to listen to my own spirit, I established an independent washing environment that requires me to walk a much different path than had become my custom.

*Toward True Worship*

> *"If your hearts can find a way to love all others without judgment, your religions could be surely set aside. For through the power of love I've shown you how to transcend all the limits of your doctrines, your philosophies and pride."*
>
> I Come (A Song of Spiritual Renaissance) - Raja

I feel the need to say that, while I appreciate the work that churches do, it's safe to say that they are used, by most, in a way synonymous with "automatic dishwashers." Quite often, we operate under the guise of honoring social collaboration inducing dictates such as the biblical scripture (Hebrews 10:25 - King James Version) which says: "Forsake not the assembling of yourselves together as the manner of some and much more as you see the day approaching." Yet, beneath a facade of spiritual commitment and dedication lies clear evidence that we have succumbed to "spiritual laziness," guilt and fear. As a consequence, we've established churches as the place we go to quiet the appeal of our soul to take full charge of building a spiritually sound base for our lives.

We have literally refused to exercise the personal discipline that would lead to the development of our inherent spiritual guidance system. The result is that, like sheep, we've become content to retreat to the cleverly fashioned grazing fields of highly dogmatic religious rhetoric. To cope with the aftertaste of having swallowed and ingested a litany of lies and half truths, we've hypnotized ourselves to become quite proficient at obeying orders and feigning joy. Having been simultaneously stripped of the truth of our identity and our confidence to know God for ourselves, we show up for our regular feeding, and chew, religiously, on the cud of self-deprecation and spiritual malaise.

Understanding that all is choice, for those of you who feel that church is needful - by all means - do church. We are each on individual paths to wholeness and inner fulfillment. It is my belief that each of us is destined to arrive at the point of standing independent of any institution for spiritual enlightenment and enrichment. When we have each traveled the long and winding road that leads to the very core of our being, we will rediscover the "fire of Godhood," which anchors our existence. It is then that we will worship at the alter of our own Self-knowing, and come to appreciate the spirituality of all people and all things. It is then that we will come to understand where and what church truly is.

Blessed and needful are those churches that are committed to helping you arrive at this point and are content to send you on your way. This will be the nature of the institutions of worship that maintain their viability and vitality in the new millennium. They will be led by souls whose love and humility will compel them to love, honor and serve all as God-beings equal to themselves. As we release our penchant for being manipulated by fear, the haughty arrogance of religious leaders who have become overblown by their own sense of significance will no longer be tolerated, and the image of the church as "the" authority on spiritual authenticity and value" will wane and dissipate.

A lack of personal willpower and discipline may require a more rigid application of discipline from without. According to your individual needs, you may choose either mild, or more abrasive detergents and tools for your dishwashing task. Your choice of scrapers, brushes, scrub pads, and dish cloths will depend upon whether you have burnt spaghetti pots and baked macaroni dishes, the regular run of glassware, flatware, china, and waterless cookware or fine china and delicate stemware. For some, the tools are distinct, exact and non-flexible, such as a literal interpretation of the Bible, and attendance at every church service and prayer meeting. Some choose a wider variety of tools, including various insights gleaned from the authors of assorted books, seminars and audio programs, along with the occasional visit to a center of worship. For others, the daily, mutually respectful interactions afforded with every of life's engagements is church enough. It's your choice. You be the judge. Just trust that as we become more gentle, loving, accepting, and trusting of ourselves and others, we will begin to require less abrasive tools for our process and, ultimately, no tools at all.

## Your Spiritual Practice

Be sure to establish an environment that your soul gets excited about; and that you invest in the tools you need for the job. As the need arises, have the courage to make adjustments. Your commitment and passion for doing a masterful job of preparing your vessel to serve will guide you along the proper path. The unfolding of your spiritual destiny is at stake, so make sure that your choice is guided by the Father, or the all-seeing eye of your inner guide.

### *Summary*

- There is basic and similar elemental truth resting at the core of every religion.
- Participation in church does not insure that you are on a path that will unfold into Spiritual Genius and Life-Mastery.
- Make sure that your participation is based on more than habit and/or someone else's expectation for you.
- A demeanor of spiritual laziness, coupled with guilt and fear have established churches as places we go to quiet the appeal of our souls to work out our own salvation.
- Be willing to adjust your spiritual practice according to the desires of your soul.
- We are evolving toward an age where, in our quest for spiritual enrichment, all will stand independent of institutions.

A Task: Take a moment to retrace the process that has brought you to your current level of spiritual understanding and expression. What is the nature of your current practice? Make a list of its attributes and the reasons this approach works for you. What tools do you use in your dishwashing experience? Are there additional tools and/or environments that you are considering as expanded possibilities? If so, what are they?

Affirmation: I establish - for my spiritual practice and self-renewal - an environment that appeals to the desires of my soul. The tools that I use deepen my experience and prepare me to reveal more of my true identity.

# Chapter 9

*Scraping Your Plate: Getting Rid of the Baggage*

*"Brethren, I count not myself to have apprehended; but this one thing I do, forgetting those things which are behind, and reaching forth unto those things which are before, I press toward the mark of the high calling of God."*

-Philippians 3:13-14

While I presume most dishwashing these days is done with the aid of an automatic dishwasher, for the purpose of this illustration and by way of personal preference, I choose to wash my dishes the "old fashioned way," by hand. This hands on approach signifies a willingness to work out my own soul salvation. In the area of interpersonal relationships, its' not unusual that our move from one experience to another is accompanied by evidence of having had unhealthy encounters, or of having processed our encounters in unhealthy ways. This evidence, commonly referred to as "baggage," is often more evident to those with whom we interact. But, most often, only in those rare moments of naked self-disclosure are we aware of it ourselves. On a vibrational level, it shows up in our attitude and general disposition toward life. It also seeps out to lace our relationships with elements of bitterness and sarcasm, which we spew at persons both old and new to our experience. This baggage is the most common influence beneath the haphazard methods and misguided motivations that typify our approach to new experiences. It is the yoke that binds us to replay unpleasant scenarios, until we discover our souls true intent. Unable to escape a continuous cycle of self-defeating behavior, it has become our habit to continually transpose the stagnant energy of bygone ordeals onto newly emerging ideals. In doing so, we virtually guarantee repeat performances of yesterday's, yesteryear's and even yesterlife's dramas.

As we engage the second step in the Tao of Dishwashing, before you place your dishes into the water, it's crucial to understand the importance of properly scraping from your plate any and all remnants of meals past.

*The Battleground of Interpersonal Relationship*

The area of life experience that accrues the most baggage is that of intimate relationships, particularly marriage. Failing to understand and honor the needs of our souls, as well as the gifts others bring in service to those needs, our relationships are - far too often - reduced to the semblance of a battlefield. The end game is that conflict and combat over getting our ego-centered needs met routinely churns out grizzly, battle-scarred, bitter veterans of relationship wars. Consequently, our lives are often laid waste with collateral damage wrought through an inordinate sense of our soul's highest objective in pairing with another.

Despite our egotistical desires and the wistful projections of some self-proclaimed romantics and romance novelists, the cover has been pulled off the commonly accepted idea that the main objective in relationships is to have someone come into our lives to "complete us," or make us whole. High levels of domestic violence, along with skyrocketing divorce rates and the lingering hostility that usually accompanies our departure from relationships provide a clear indication that this is not happening. Yet, in lieu of delving to our core to engage the dance our soul is doing, we endeavor - time and again - to re-make the same bed, by having another commit to remain beside us in a lifetime of co-dependent repose. We do so even when all indications are that each of our souls says otherwise. As a result of not having our expectations met, we've engaged the "war of the sexes" - a psychological, spiritual, emotional, physical, and financial gender conflict and ego-bashing of major proportions.

Counted among its casualties are many women who find themselves deeply entrenched in a "there are no good men left out there/I can do bad all by myself" mentality, as well as many men who have processed their experiences in a way that has brought them to the place of seeing women as the "weaker sex" and, therefore, subject to men. With visions of snaring a "trophy wife, some only see beautiful and decorative playthings that are to be fondled, flaunted and placed on display alongside other conquests. For others, bitterness and a quiet hatred has brought them to considering women as no more than objects intended for the fulfillment of their sexual desires.

## Getting Rid of Baggage

Organized religion has done its bit to found, ground, bind, and support this conflict. Along with various scripture put forth to cement the submissive role of women, we've bought into the "Eve in the Garden" syndrome and similar tales of woe that cast women as subversive. This has led to a subconscious typecasting that has, if but inadvertantly, regulated women to a subordinate status. The result is that, during this time of deeply impacting change, the male ego is disconsolate. The reason for this is that, at a deep level of its collective psyche, the male ego is grappling, at a deeper level, with suspicions surrounding what the female ego is "up to." These suspicions and the internal conflict they engender are responsible for why you hear the labels "bitch" and "ho" bantered about to the extent they are. It is also responsible for the distasteful phenomenon that we refer to as "gay bashing."

Clear that it faces the final phases of its supreme domination over human affairs, the male ego senses that the female essence (replete with its core, nurturing qualities of love, compassion and forgiveness) is on the rise. At the crux of this rise is the fear of the displacement of its authoritarian rule. Dare I say that the male ego archetype is not of the mindset to handle this transition gracefully. In fact, under the guise of paying homage and feigning appreciation, it has hosted a party on her behalf. Yet, this party has become quite a dismissive affair, as the "party-favors" clearly denote that the male ego is having no part of female energy flaunting itself in any fashion. Well, I might add that there are notable exceptions to this intolerance - unless in the form of a scantily-clad, seductive body wearing hot pants, a G-string, bikini, or nothing at all. One thing is for sure, she had best not show up flaunting her intelligence and a sense of self-authority.

At the root of the dilemma is the female ego asserting itself in broad strokes. She is preparing the way for the feminine spiritual essence to initiate an age that will usher energies that promote balance and healing in our realm. The challenge for the ego-driven male psyche is its resentment at the prospect of "decreasing that she (the feminine essence) might increase." The fear is that of a significance, through the loss of identity and, thus, the loss of power. Consequently, the male ego is stuck within the confines of old paradigm thinking. It is utterly unaware that the promise of this dawning new age is that of the proper integration of the masculine and feminine energies within us all. So, it can think of no better response than to put up a fight. Operating within this realm of consciousness with this set of gender expectations, there is literally no chance for building a meaningful relationship that has the potential for maintaining its value long after it has changed its form.

Rarely do we allow the nature of our intimate/sexual relationships to change without assigning blame, by pointing the finger at the other party or resigning to having "made a mistake" in our choice of partners. We would do well to consider that regardless of how deep the drama and sinister the characters, the theme of the central plot of our life is never about another person. It is all about you or me, and the unique and distinct requirements of our spiritual growth. Processing our experiences through filters clogged with expectations and judgment, we fail to see that the same person with whom we were enamored, overjoyed and deeply in love on the day we consummated our bond - the person who came into our lives to facilitate our growth, by helping us to discover and strengthen our weak points - never wavered from the task.

Though bound to the same processing modalities as we, they may have often switched costumes and demeanors. They may have chosen to alternate between the overtly loving, nurturing and supportive soul-mate and the intensely demonstrative, volatile and highly believable "devil's advocate." Even so, their contribution to our lives was intended to incite us to a greater and more wholesome relationship with ourselves. They came to prompt us into seeing ourselves more clearly in the mirror of introspection and self-analysis. Their soul, as well as ours is and remains certain that seeing ourselves clearly and loving ourselves dearly is the direct and unencumbered path to the sense of union we seek with another. And that is why they came. It's important to note that this "God-service" and "holy contribution" was never intended to be at the expense of either party. It's only our coveted sense of loss that prohibits us from seeing the inherent and overriding benefit derived from every relationship we engage.

In that our enrollment in interpersonal relationship provides the greatest yet most challenging opportunity to see ourselves more clearly, and to be loved into compliance with our heart's desire, each of us has accumulated an abundance of the "frequent flyer miles of repeated experience." Consequently, we've shared periods of grief around not having arrived at a satisfactory destination or place to call "home." This sense of futility resonates not only in the area of intimate relationship, but also in the areas of spirituality and career or life-purpose. Know that the journey home is an inward journey and, if we are to arrive at the gate of the "Kingdom," we must muster the courage to rise up, again, and take flight - even in inclement weather. So, after having pulled up a chair to the table of a particular life experience and eaten our fill, it's needful that we clear our plate, in order to prepare for the next experience.

The first step is for you to claim your baggage. In order to do so, you must first accept that the plate is yours and that there are remnants of food on it that only you are responsible for clearing. You may be experiencing the pain of an intimate relationship with family or friends that - due to some level of disappointment, betrayal or distrust - has long since shifted. You may be harboring the deeply hidden and utterly embarrassing details of a deprived or abusive childhood. An employment matter may have left you feeling passed-over, slighted or otherwise violated. Or, maybe it's the pain of deeply-seated despair and disillusionment, born of a religious experience that hurt you to the depths of your soul. Or, is the haunting frustration of failing time and time again to manifest your dreams causing you to remain bitter, stuck and, maybe, unemployed?

Whether singular or plural, you know what the issues are. You are also aware of when and how they arrived on your plate as well as whether you were dining alone or in the company of a significant other. You sat at the table of their experience and ate your fill. And, now, even though you've left the table, you bring your doggy bag with those remnants to every subsequent meal you ingest. As bitterness, anger, resentment, fear, and the desire for retaliation, they have set up shop in your body, soul and mind. They are poised to reveal themselves as chaos and disease, unless you release them and let them go.

Accept that the first step in preparing to receive the blessing of alignment with your life purpose is to release the obvious thing(s) that hinder the growth of your soul. You've got to literally scour your soul or "scrape your plate," by making the commitment to move beyond the influence of things that no longer serve your growth. So consider these impediments, now, for the final time. It's time to release them and let them go so the process of renewal can begin. Start by forgiving yourself for keeping these things on your plate until they began to rot, gather mold and stink up your life. Then forgive the person(s) or experience(s), and accept that neither came into your life to dis-empower you. Finally realize that they only invited you over for dinner, or offered to take you out to dine. The choices of selecting from the menu and deciding how much to eat were yours. Even if they offered to order for you or spoon feed you, you could have politely or otherwise refused. You also had no obligation to clean your plate, even if you or they felt it appropriate, given they were paying the tab. You could have eaten what you desired, said, "No more," and made a conscious decision to pass on the rest. So, it's time to move on. Release them to their next highest good and prepare to move forward to yours. There is no longer any need for you to feel vulnerable and afraid.

You can trust that a healthy sense of self-love carries with it a built in protection device that will prohibit you from giving your power away and/or making yourself needlessly vulnerable. This awareness will provide a fail-safe against processing future experiences as attempts to divest you of your right to self-determination. Trust the wisdom of your soul to usher you into alignment with the next, best, highest opportunity for healthy relationships, in all areas of your life.

# Getting Rid of the Baggage

## *Summary*

- It is a common tendency to carry the baggage of anger, resentment, presumed failure, disappointment, and plain old fear from one experience to another.
- This baggage becomes stuck on our plates (within our consciousness), where it festers, molds, rots, and stinks up our lives.
- This baggage shows up in the form of disease in our emotional, mental and physical bodies.
- Our penchant for blaming others for our pain blinds us to the real causes, and ultimately renders us too bitter and proud to acknowledge that our pain is "self-induced."
- The area of interpersonal relationships provides our greatest opportunities for growth and, thus, creates the greatest amount of baggage in our lives.
- The expectations that we place on our relationships cause us to miss the true gifts they bring.
- Though our partner's methods often vary, their soul's commitment to the objectives of our souls never does.
- The people who came into our lives to engage us in relationship only invited us over for dinner or out to dine.
- The notion, that we were "force fed," is our own private illusion, constructed to keep us from facing ourselves, squarely in the mirror of self-observation.
- We have each accumulated enough "frequent flyer miles of repeated experience" to have an intimate awareness of every piece of baggage that we own.
- By "scraping your plate," you can remove the obvious barriers to your success and happiness from your life.

A Task: Consider the resentments you have carried around that have festered and grown into physical and emotional impediments to your well-being. Take a walk over to the garbage can of physical, emotional, psychological, and spiritual release; and make the conscious decision to "scrape your plate."

Affirmation: "I release and I let go of the pain and resentment of presumed failures, disappointments, and hurts of the past. I remove these issues from my plate, and am prepared to begin anew, with a fresh perspective and new attitude."

# Chapter 10

*Pre-Rinsing - The Process of Introspection and Self-Observation*

*"I've already started on a new point of view, seeing things I've never seen before. There are no limits to the things that I can do; I've escaped from my revolving door."*

The Voices of Change - Raja

A sure way to be drawn back into undesirable physical, emotional, psychological, and spiritual conditions is to not have clarity about what drew us there in the first place. Having made the decision to release the baggage of the past, it's now important to assess the motivating factors (those, quite often, hidden instigators) that attract undesirable conditions into our lives.

I heard a story about a man who unknowingly came upon a large hole while walking down the street. Paying no attention, he fell in. After spending a great deal of time and energy climbing out, feeling quite angry, he reasoned it wasn't his fault - that he didn't know the hole was there. Walking down the same street a few days later, he reasoned that he would maneuver around the hole. Having no sense that the area surrounding the hole was unstable, he fell, again, into this enormously large hole. Emerging somewhat tattered, he attributed his plight to "bad luck," and continued on his way. A third time, he walked the same street. Determined to find a way to get past this hole, he fell in once more. Pulling himself up and feeling somewhat chagrined, he arrived at the well-earned conclusion that this was all his doing; that his misappropriated persistence was to blame and that tomorrow he would "take a different road."

I share this story because it's common that even after emerging from the ditch, scraping ourselves off and, ultimately, deciding to "take a different road," the residual memory of former behavioral patterns continues to plague our consciousness. To the detriment of our souls, as faint shadows, their physical, emotional and psychological imprints remain on our plate. It is the process of introspection and self-observation that provides the opportunity to discover, evaluate, eliminate, and replace ways of thinking that spur emotional reactions that keep us mired in conditions that no longer serve our growth.

## Your "Achilles Heel"

> "Let us lay aside every weight, and the sin which doth easily beset us."
>
> —Hebrews 12:1

There is a story in Greek mythology of Achilles, son of Peleus and Thetis, and foremost hero of the Trojan War. Thetis, his mother, attempted to make him immortal by bathing him in the river Styx, but the heel she held remained vulnerable. Hearing from Peleus that Achilles was fated to die at Troy, Thetis disguised him as a girl and hid him at Skyros. He was found by his friend, Odysseus, who persuaded him to go to war. At Troy, he quarreled with Agamemnon, and sulked in his tent until his friend Patroclus was killed by Hector. Filled with grief and rage, Achilles slew Hector and dragged his body to the Greek camp. He was later killed by Paris, who wounded him in his heel.

Just as I am sure that each of us comes into the world with unique gifts, talents and destinies, I am certain that, on our way to Mastery, we each bring a unique set of challenges or potentially undermining tendencies that we are charged with overcoming. Given a commitment to growth, if we have exercised any degree of self-assessment in our lives, we can narrow these challenges down to a few or one particularly nagging tendency. A little self-assessment will disclose this as the "thing or things" that trip us up more readily than any others. These challenges run the gamut, ranging from a tendency to overly depend on others to an unwillingness to flow with others, due to an overblown sense of selfishness and/or independence. They may entail the need to seek validation and approval from others or an incessant desire to control others behavior through emotional and psychological one-upmanship. Your challenge may even pertain to a penchant for bullying others through financial and/or physical intimidation or manipulation.

## The Process of Introspection and Self-Observation

Your particular Achilles Heel may manifest as a self-righteous attitude that sets you at odds with those who don't share your views. It may be that you feel you will only become complete when you find the perfect mate. As a result, you've decided to refrain from relationships until the "perfect person" comes along. Or you may feel that you can only become successful when you've obtained all the information available about a particular field of endeavor. Consequently, you find yourself on a never-ending search for knowledge, never taking the risk to apply what you've already learned. Or maybe you'll have to dig, as I did, through several layers of illusion, or venture back to your childhood to find your particular challenge. The possibilities are as endless as our potential for seeing ourselves as less than whole and complete.

Quite often, our ability to disguise our true motive or operate without conscious awareness of it precludes our ability to clearly see how we are operating in the world. For instance, during my first marriage, feeling that her impact would be greater felt if she focused on the children, I resisted the idea of my wife working. Though she was working when we met, had worked with me in my business endeavors and was willing to work, I was perfectly willing to work as long and hard as needed to support my family. What I wasn't clear about is that I was working hard to support my hidden desire. I'm sure that seeing my mother struggle to raise a family while working two jobs, coupled with my desire to be the provider for my family had a lot to do with it. Yet, I must confess that these were not my primary motivations. Even though my church indoctrination provided cover for my private aims, the truth is that my ego had arisen to protect (control) her from exposure to the prying and prodding that I projected onto potential male-dominated work environments.

Reaching back even further, from early on, I established a reputation among the adults in my community as the boy who was going to "be something." Even today, when I return home, I am esteemed and highly respected. I was the "self-motivated one," who routinely canvassed the neighborhood for odd jobs, and made runs to the store for the neighbors. My hope was that "you can keep the change" meant I would have enough money to buy a "whole-lotta-candy." As a teenager, in the spring, summer and fall, I would chop weeds, white-wash garages and fences and wash cars. I would rise early in the winter to shovel snowy sidewalks and driveways. Yes sir, everybody knew I would make it. That is every body except my stepfather. As hard as I worked and as respectful as I was, he often told me - in mostly angry and never uncertain terms - that "just like my daddy, I would never be sh---!" - well, you know!" It was quite painful for me to have this man whom I loved and respected brand my life with the stamp of failure. After all, I was just a boy who was willing to work hard, and who felt he had a promising life ahead of him.

After leaving home, at age seventeen, though I lived just a few miles away and rarely stopped by, I made a point of showing up to share the news of my new job with Goodyear Tire & Rubber, as a machinist apprentice. I was thrilled to discover that my starting income was greater than what he was currently making, after almost 20 years on the job. Oh, I should mention the visit I made to show off my first new car, a 1974 Grand Torino (Brougham) Coupe, which I purchased at age 20. It was nicely equipped with a tilt steering wheel, cruise control, (padded) Landau Roof, factory chrome wheels, a 400 cubic inch engine, 60/40 split seats, AM FM stereo, and air conditioning. I had also gotten married and was the proud father of a bouncing baby boy!

Now, I'm sure that, at first blush, it appears my aim was to wag my finger in my stepfather's face and say "Now, who ain't gone be nothin'?" However, the reality is that, at this point, I was only seeking to gain his approval and to have him repudiate his prior assessment of me. I felt that it was so necessary for him to validate my worth...that his approval would aid me in feeling good about my chances of making it in the world. It wasn't until years later, while engaged in an intense inner struggle that all of this began to resurface for me. At that time, though we had reconciled years later, before he passed on, I became quite angry with him about his assessment and treatment of me. We made our peace in 1977, about four years before he passed on. Yet, here I was - in, I'd say, 1983 - totally "hell-bent" on disproving his assessment of my potential. Here I was, still attempting to rinse the residue of the brand of failure he inscribed on my plate in my childhood.

Years earlier, while he was alive, I began taking entrepreneurial risks that were based on good ideas, but less than sound motives. I felt the need to "get my name up in lights" as soon as possible so that his words could stop haunting me. He passed on before I could accomplish it, and I was hurt and angry. As a result, I created what I have in the past referred to as near misses - or those pursuits that almost pan out and

## The Process of Introspection and Self-Observation

provide that often elusive break-through but, for some reason, fall just short of the mark.

In lieu of more details, the story could end here with my stepfather being considered a "bad" and "very angry" man, and me an unwelcome if not abused child with an understandably low self-esteem. I could add the exhortation that you and I are worthy of success and should never allow ourselves to be motivated by someone's negative assessment of what we can or cannot, will or will never do. I could close the chapter, but that would not be the "end of story."

Upon closer self-examination, I discovered that my Achilles Heel was not the need to have my stepfather's or anyone else's approval. My unique challenge involved a subconscious desire to overly depend on others to do things for me that I could and should do for myself, including making my own decisions and maintaining the strength of my convictions. Even though I never showed a lack of these traits in my youth, with his incessant badgering and in his unique and inordinate way, my stepfather literally jump-started me onto the path of independence. The methods he used were mostly harsh and could have sponsored negative and more harmful consequences. They ultimately did not, because my conscious choice was to respond to them with my ability to remain focused on being the best person I knew how to be. I chose to remain respectful. And, though I was not afraid or intimidated by him, I chose to not strike back at him either verbally or physically.

There were times when it appeared we were headed for the ultimate showdown. I literally felt that my life was at stake. So, I began to build my body, by lifting homemade barbells thrown together by adding concrete blocks to the ends of a broom stick. I would also hoist my brothers, Anthony and Bryon, on each of my shoulders, and run around the house as many times as I could. During another period, after I was hit in the back of my head with the telephone receiver, I began wearing a hunting knife on my belt. But, fortunately, the showdown never occurred. My sense of respect for humanity at large and him as my parent, as well as my personal integrity and perseverance helped me to not only endure, but to not consider myself a victim. It was this stand that, ultimately, salvaged our relationship.

On the few occasions when I've shared the details of my relationship with my stepfather with others, there have been those who've attempted to get me to admit that I hated him. That is not the case. Even as a child,

I thought it quite interesting that I did not hate him, but loved and respected him. Though hard fought to gain, that which he brought to my life - that which I can finally see in our interaction - is priceless to my journey. And I am grateful to him for it.

Even though the business decisions I made appeared to be born of less than positive motivations, they yielded clear benefits. They were, of their own design, intended for moving me in directions for gaining much needed skills. Moving forward, these skills have helped to forge a path of self-sustenance and independence. They were not the destination at all and, thus, were not "near misses." They were needful stops along an ever-unfolding road, leading to the unfolding of my divine purpose. Though, at one point, I thought one of those endeavors ("Expert Auto Cleaning") was at the root of my destiny, the many years I spent operating this auto detailing business trained me to focus on and master the details - to search the nooks and crannies for any deposits that may escape the topical view or that may be hard to reach. It's clear, even as it pertains to writing this book, that garnered the intended benefits of that experience, incorporated them into my life and, though somewhat disappointed, I moved on.

My experience as a remodeling contractor has given me the opportunity to become and remain mindful of the principle of "due process," while taking an idea from its inception through each stage required to bring it into manifestation. To share the lesson in as few words as possible, I generally work alone. In committing to acquire skills in all the trades, I learned the values of patience, practical application and order. Making a commitment to do as much as I could for and by myself, each of these experiences provided me with valuable skills and life lessons. And, in a more meaningful way, each has been paramount in helping me to eradicate my Achilles Heel.

## Creating a "Collective Achilles Heel"

It is also possible for the consciousness of a group to create a "collective Achilles heel," which has the potential for affecting, to some extent, every member of the group. Such is the case with those who believe that another group or some outside force has the power to determine their destiny. When we choose to defer our power of self-determination to another entity, we do a couple of things that obscure our ability to comprehend the truth of our circumstances, and ultimately rise above them.

## The Process of Introspection and Self-Observation

The first effect of engaging this "us versus them" struggle for a fair share of the resources, is to disconnect ourselves from the natural flow and unbiased distribution of the universal source of good. We do so by adopting a demeanor of defensiveness and manipulation. This posture refutes the clear evidence of natural order and unlimited, universal supply. We are, in essence, saying that man (ego, personality, intellect, and flesh) is an abandoned species that is left entirely to its own devices. This belief system leaves us fearing that he with the cleverest devices or with the greatest proficiency with those devices will, ultimately, rule the day.

Second, by establishing some "Goliath" as an obstacle that must be restrained or destroyed in order for us to enjoy our rightful share of the kingdom, we engage in a skirmish that dilutes our creative energies. This happens because we inadvertently divert them into reinforcing this illusion. By doing so, we manifest and sustain this adopted reality with the energy of our own belief systems. The end result is to regulate ourselves to a self-created, subservient and compliant role in the shaping of our collective fate.

For those of you who tout a legally enforced value called "affirmative action," I support that there is a karmic influence that, beyond doubt, requires a balancing of the scales of injustice. With that comes the consideration of whether we have forgotten the source of our power to create our lives on an equal footing. While my sense is that there is no "wrestling among the Gods" for equal dispensation of resources among the races of people on planet Earth, my caution is to seek justice while not becoming attached to a historical sense of victimhood. To do otherwise may cause you to place a psychological governor on your self-worth and creative potential.

Now, it's perfectly allowable to continue administering mouth to mouth resuscitation to this and a myriad of dying collective consciousness paradigms. Yet, it's very important to note that a commitment to discovering the true source of power will open our eyes to the clear reality that our own consciousness - individual and collective - constitutes the only prison with any power to hold us captive. Consider that promotion does not come from without, but from within. When we become willing to release ourselves from limited, divisive, outmoded, adversarial social constructs, the spiritual energies constituting (giving life to) our true nature will open our eyes to the truth. The truth is that, within the realm of Grace and Truth - there are neither minorities nor majorities, only God Being. When we embrace this truth, these powers will become fully engaged, and work through us to manifest our Mastery and Genius. It is then that we will witness the power and impact of our individual contribution to the aggregate "kingdom of heaven on earth."

*"Be Ye transformed by the renewing of your mind."*

- Romans 12:2

This quote, attributed to Walter Benjamin, a German critic and philosopher (1892-1940), speaks of self-knowledge in a way that is synonymous with the pre-rinsing stage of The Tao of Dishwashing. Gleaned from "A Berlin Chronicle," and written in 1932, he states:

> "He who seeks to approach his own buried past must conduct himself like a man digging. He must not be afraid to return, again and again to the same matter; to scatter it as one scatters earth, to turn it over as one turns over soil. For the matter, itself, is but a deposit, a stratum, which yields only to the most meticulous examination what constitutes the real treasure hidden within the earth: the images severed from all others as associations that stand - like precious fragments or torsos in a collector's gallery - in the prosaic rooms of our later understanding."

In order to fully benefit from this phase of the Tao of Dishwashing, it is important that we take time to go inside. We must allow the "One who knows" to reinterpret those experiences that we have, heretofore, considered to be of no positive benefit. By releasing our attachment to old interpretations and the need to assign blame, we welcome the process of renewal, and eliminate the potential for repeating undesirable cycles. Take some time to get quiet, and allow the hot yet invigorating water of the spirit to rinse over your consciousness, renew your mind, and reveal the traps and pitfalls that have caused you to misinterpret key events in your life. Be still, while the illusions of victimization are rinsed away; freeing you to prepare for complete life transformation.

# The Process of Introspection and Self-Observation

## *Summary*

- A lack of awareness of "cause" is the surest path to repeating undesirable "effects."

- Quite often, our misappropriated energies - fueled by our insistence on doing things a certain way - cause us to fall, time and again, into the same old ditch.

- Our lack of self-awareness causes us to develop an "Achilles Heel," or point of vulnerability that is the source of repeated frustration and self-demise.

- Groups of individuals who hold similar beliefs about themselves often create a "collective Achilles Heel" which affects, to some extent, every member of the group.

- Deferring power over our lives to other persons inhibits our ability to drink equally from a free-flowing, non-biased, universal fountain of good.

- Our attachment to fixed interpretations often prevents us from seeing what is "really" going on.

- The process of introspection and detached, non-judgmental self-observation can reveal and heal those areas of vulnerability that have historically undermined our progress.

- Taking the action to affirm our true identity will connect us with Source and engage our power to manifest our creative desires.

- In the realms of higher spiritual light and understanding, there are no Black, Native American or Oriental Gods wrestling - in some spiritual realm - with White Gods over equal dispensation of the resources in the earth realm among her peoples.

A Task: Take time to think back over your life and consider what might be your Achilles Heel. Are you able to identify, with clarity, those things that have habitually led you down the same path and undermined your progress? Who are those people you may have overlooked, who clearly came to your path to help you discover and strengthen your weak points? What disguises did they wear? Can you see them in the light of their true service? What gifts did they bring to your life? Can you truly love them and thank them for their assistance?

Affirmation: (For more clarity, you may desire to substitute the name of an individual or individuals.)

"I thank everyone and everything that has shown up in my life. I allow the spirit of mind renewal to rinse away the illusion that they came to harm me. With complete clarity, I accept the full benefit of the gift they came to give."

# Chapter 11

*Preparing the Water: Engaging the Spirit*

*"I know thy works that they art neither hot nor cold. I would thou wert cold or hot. So then because thou art lukewarm, and neither cold nor hot, I will spue thee out of my mouth."*

-Revelations 3:15-16

As we move through this book and do the work, I trust that you are having a wonderful journey and gaining both practical benefit and inspiration. The word "inspiration" is at the center of the process of preparing the water, for water is my analogy for spirit. We are preparing to "get in-the-spirit. The process of preparing the water speaks to the level of excitement, enthusiasm and passion you generate as you clear the space for your Genius and Mastery to unfold. Remember - the greater your level of passion and connectedness with each aspect of your life experience (i.e. the hotter the water), the more invigorated your soul becomes. The hotter the water, the more you, potentially, experience leaps and bounds in your growth process.

There is another childhood story to share. This one involves a dishwashing assignment I inherited from my mother's younger sister, Aunt Frances. When I was maybe eight years old, Aunt Frances and her daughters, Terry and Sherry, lived with us. True to my mother's nature, if you were a household regular, she found something for you to do. She was very much into the idea of shared responsibility. On this occasion, Aunt Frances' task was to wash the dishes. And, like most, she sought to pawn that task off. As it turned out, I became the pawn. I don't remember how much it cost her or what she promised, but I do remember her standing over me in a supervisory role while I did the work. Even though she farmed the job out to me, they were her dishes, and she wanted to make sure I did the job right. You see, that's the kind of effect momma had on folk.

I was washing away, when I felt the thump of Aunt Frances' finger on the back of my head, which made for a nice "thumping block," thanks to its shape and one of my momma's fresh, custom haircuts. Aunt Frances seeme to have a problem with my technique. In fact, while ranting about the lukewarm water (which I thought was hot), she snatched the dish rag from my hand. She complained that I was not getting the job done. She said something about the plates having enough grease left on them to "fry a chicken." Well, not only was I disappointed that my work was rejected, but I didn't receive any compensation for the effort I put forth to that point.

As did Aunt Frances, your soul knows that lukewarm water, or an attitude of indifference and disconnectedness, is not sufficient for dissolving the greasy remnants of a lifetime of mediocrity and discontent. As my dishwashing was rejected without reward, so are works fueled by anything less than passion, which I refer to as hot water or "the fire of God." This is that "fire in the belly" level of commitment, determination and connectedness that is stirred by your understanding of and desire to meet the requirements for building a Master Soul. As you press toward the mark of your highest calling, the attitude with which you pursue your life purpose must convey your commitment to doing all things with a spirit of passion and delight. As the fuel that propels a student of Life-Mastery, this energy must grade out at nothing less than an (A) in the categories of effort, attitude and commitment.

Passion compels us to raise our sights, so that our level of self-expectation no longer hovers around the (C to C+) standard of merely surviving or doing what it takes to "get by." Quite often, due to the way we process the events in our lives, when it is the will of God that we are blazing flames of fire, the flame of desire (the flame of the Father) dwindles to pilot light status. Our largely subconscious yet habitual practice of sending ourselves dis-empowering messages through our words, thoughts, feelings, and body language impedes the flow of energy from our center. The accumulative result is that we become jaded, indifferent and disconnected from the source of our passion. We also begin to discount the people and events with which we interact on a daily basis. This lukewarm disposition or lack of joy is a forerunner to the energy of depression and other mental disease, whose subtle effects plague untold millions. At times, safeguarding against the short-circuiting of our peace of mind, enthusiasm and overall well being requires a more methodical or disciplined approach. Unless you are able to utilize the energy of passion to accomplish and maintain your balance, the intensity generated by the circumstances we face during these shifting times will prove difficult to process. If you find the flame of your desire burning at less than satisfactory levels, here are a few stacks of kindlin' to help you to pump it up.

*Monitoring Your "Self-Talk"*

The most significant practice I can recommend is to make a conscious effort to monitor and adjust the nature of your "self talk." We send messages to our subconscious minds every moment of our lives. The energies are encoded in our thoughts and emotions, as well as the messages conveyed in our words to ourselves and to others about ourselves. Quite often adjustments are needed to create and maintain the integrity of our private and collective worlds. So, it is of utmost importance to maintain moment-by moment mindfulness of how you are programming your subconscious mind.

*"Be ye transformed by the renewing of your mind"*

Romans 12:2

*The Two Most Powerful Words in the Universe*

It is a little known, yet optimally powerful secret that the two most powerfully creative words in the Universe when combined are "I" and "AM." As a personal declaration, when taken together, these words generate the consummate energy, fire or creative/destructive essence of God. They are as creatively basic, raw and elemental as the process of rubbing two sticks together to ignite a flame. They are as uproarious, unbridled and all-consuming as the lava of an erupting volcano. They are as dynamic, restorative and life-sustaining as the very breath of life. They are also at your command. We all use them - though in largely unconsciously ways - many times everyday. Use them wisely.

When the indiscriminate cosmic forces that create our world hear the words "I AM," they immediately engage their creative/destructive energies to bring to pass whatever we attach to this command. Herein lies the wisdom of Proverbs 23:7 (King James Bible) which states: "As he thinketh in his heart, so is he." Whatever we think, speak, or feel as the truth about ourselves and our set of circumstances or life in general, is obliged to manifest in our world - at some point...in some form. The how, when and where are determined by the strength of our conviction or lack thereof. If you say to yourself "I Am stupid, inadequate or unattractive," there is virtually no hope of your projecting an aura of intelligence, aptitude or inner/outer beauty to your creative forces, to others or to yourself. If you are in the habit of thinking your situation hopeless and feeling things will never get better, though you appear an image of positivity and speak the language of a believer in better things, you are destined to, at best, draw lukewarm water from the fountains of life. Engage this process of duality or complacency long enough, and you will be found floating face-down in an emotional cesspool of self pity. A spiritual autopsy will reveal that your remains are festering with the acidic and parasitic bacteria of demise through self-loathing.

You can only draw hot water or have a true sense of enthusiasm, connectedness and passion when the energies of your thoughts, feelings, words, and deeds are in alignment. Any evidence of inconsistency concerning your truth about yourself or your circumstances or desires will show up as mediocrity in key areas of your life. To ensure that they don't emerge to unexpectedly derail your progress, latent pockets of these energies, which have remained dormant for years, must be purged from your consciousness and your physical body. One method I have found to be particularly helpful for generating positive self-talk involves the use of affirmations. Depending upon the reinforcement I am seeking, I create and utilize a maximum of three affirmations at a time. I have found it beneficial to write them on 3x5 index cards and to carry them around with me everyday. They are always worded in a way that emphasizes the positive result I desire rather than focusing on eliminating an undesirable condition. For instance, if I desire to improve my health and vitality by exercising to eliminate excessive weight and stress, I would create an affirmation which might say: "I am engaged in an exercise program that I am excited about! My body gladly receives the benefits of increased vitality, greater flexibility, improved circulation, and strength." Or I could say: "I am 20 pounds lighter and feeling great about it."

For adjustments in my eating habits I could say: "I eat those things which support my vision of self as a completely balanced and healthy person." If finances are a concern, I could create an affirmation which says: "I am an integral part of an abundant universe. Money comes to me in avalanches of abundance." Once you have created your affirmations, I recommend repeating them with passion and conviction at least three times a day for twenty-one days. I recommend: (1) In the morning, just after awakening - so that your mind will have these thoughts with which to begin the day; (2) Sometime in the middle of the day, between lunch and 2:00 PM - to give yourself a much needed boost and (3) Just before going to sleep - which may prove the most critical time of all. Your subconscious mind engages in a tremendous amount of activity during your sleeping hours. Therefore, feed it the quality of information that will work toward bringing your desires into manifestation. The twenty-one day period has been suggested as the amount of time it takes for your subconscious mind to override old programming and integrate new beliefs. The more you use these affirmations, the more effective they will become as a tool for reversing the drain on your life force. In order to attract the quality of experience you desire for your life, learn to monitor your self-talk, and send your creative forces messages that enhance your life and boost your physical, emotional, mental, and spiritual vitality.

Affirmation:
I speak to myself in ways that reveal the truth of my being. The truth is that I AM brilliant and fully capable of shining as brightly as I desire in any aspect of life I choose.

*An Attitude of Gratitude*

I've experienced times when I found it hard to "count my blessings." Focusing on the unpleasant aspects of my life caused them to overshadow everything else. Not surprisingly, it became difficult for me to muster a glimmer of hope or gratitude for anything. I soon realized that the more I wallowed in feelings of lack, anger, disappointment, and self-pity, the more burdensome and engrossing those conditions became. So, I learned to "take the air out of the unfavorable appearances," by feeding them righteous energy, or the energy of "right thinking." The simplest way I found to do this is by expressing simple, yet deeply felt gratitude. I learned to release my expectations of how a "good life" should flow. I took time out to connect with my true motives or what I was really after. I began to relate with the truth of how everything that showed up on my path came to support my pursuit of self-discovery and Life-Mastery.

Therefore, there was nothing for me to fret about. This released me to harness my creative energies to establish a more productive flow with the changes that were occurring in my life. To signal your appreciation for circumstances that promote your pursuit of life-mastery, make a daily habit of taking five minutes to pull aside and do nothing but thank the spark of life for indwelling your soul.

As one of my most valuable and prized assets, I have also found it important to utilize my sense of humor. The abilities to remain committed to positive change (despite appearances) and to find humor in my challenges, have been saving graces for me. In deciding that I was not a victim, I also concluded that the events, situations and conditions that came to my life were never designed to victimize or destroy me. In accepting that life was "for me" and not "against me," I began to work on going with the flow, while processing my growth opportunities in a way that worked for rather than against me. I realized that there was no "devil" for me to battle, and that the only battle is an internal one - a battle with a false sense of self. This understanding caused me to conclude that, where the aims of my soul are concerned, I AM the predestined winner! I encourage you to seek out a clearing beyond the clutter of unmitigated life circumstance and, from the sincerity of your heart, pronounce your gratitude to life for continuing to sponsor your efforts to shape your unique destiny and fulfill your purpose.

Affirmation of Gratitude:

"Spirit of Life, I give thanks for the spark that ignites my breathing, heart beat, the circulation of my blood, the movement of my limbs, the function of all my organs, and that constitutes the creative energy that I AM. From the depths of my heart and soul, I offer simple gratitude for all that I AM, and all that I experience in my quest for Life Mastery."

*Moving Your Body*

Exercising provides another process for lifting the clouds of emotional stagnation and gaining an energy boost or physical restoration. As spiritual beings having a human experience, we have several bodies. The physical, emotional, mental, and causal bodies are integrated and designed to work in balance and harmony. It's no secret that the conditioning of our physical body (or lack thereof) has a direct impact on our emotional, mental and spiritual bodies and, thus, our overall well-being.

## Engaging the Spirit

Quite often, our lives fail to flow as we would like because we lack overall balance. Though we consider ourselves balanced in a particular area (for instance, we may consider ourselves spiritually attuned), we take little thought for the care of our physical body as a temple for the Spirit. As custodians of these spiritual temples, it's commonplace for us to give them less care than we would the physical building where we worship. This imbalance manifests in ways that disrupt the natural integration and optimal potential of all our bodies or energy fields.

Mindful that we are preparing a "holy place," in preparation for worship service, we would reverently go about the task of dusting, vacuuming, and sanitizing our physical environment. The same holds true if we were to invite the minister to come dine at our home. We would be certain to ensure that our environment reflected an atmosphere of holiness or peace and tranquility. We might incorporate the use of air fresheners or incense to condition the atmosphere to our liking. Yet, we seem to take little to no thought that our bodies are the dwelling place of the Spirit of the Most High. We eat, drink and smoke to excess, while giving no thought to our body's need for exercise, a plentiful intake of water and oxygen, and other nutrients that contribute to routine maintenance.

Our cells are the processing centers for the activity that emanates from the various levels of our being. Kid ourselves if we must, but the fulfillment of the yearning within our souls to unfold into Mastery requires the willing cooperation of all finely-tuned aspects of our being. When this is not happening, we are bound to feel less than emotionally charged. In fact, we are bound to feel less than adequate. Until we commit to being in balance, by tending to the needs of each aspect of our integrated body, our attempt to disembark the roller-coaster of emotional enchantment and instability will prove futile. As we forever find ourselves in pursuit of stimulants and anti-depressants, the evidence pointing to our imbalance will continue to mount. If you are not incorporating some form of physical exercise into your life process, I recommend you do so. The benefits to your overall well-being of a brisk walk around the block, a daily bicycle ride, a game of tennis, or an occasional visit to the gym or spa are well worth the effort.

From another perspective on "moving your body," the periodic practice of purging your system (through adjusting your diet, utilizing an appropriate fast, or cleaning your colon) holds untold benefits for your overall health. It will prove invaluable to your ability to tune your cells to hold the vibration needed to receive the highest guidance from within.

"Affirmation:
I engage my body in physical exercise, to honor it for supporting my pursuit of life purpose. I maintain its overall health by bringing all hidden issues to the surface, where I clear them; once and for all."

*Sitting Still*

One of the most invigorating and yet difficult things for humans to do is to sit still in a quiet space for five minutes, absent the need to do anything else. No listening to music, no deliberate thinking, no doodling - nothing. While I understand how sitting in quiet stillness without an agenda might seem a gross waste of time, at critical junctures along the way, it can be the most productive thing you can do. During times of heightened stress or physical fatigue, I've found sitting still and being quiet an invaluable method for overcoming lethargic physical and emotional states. Just a few minutes have proved effective for energizing my mind and spirit. It's clear that, at a spiritual level, our resistance to sitting alone is born of a fear of facing ourselves in the mirror of reflection and introspection. At the root of the issue is not having arrived at the point of loving ourselves enough to enjoy our own company. Therefore, we are certainly not interested in granting ourselves an exclusive interview. This tendency prompts the need for constant companionship, in one form or another. Choosing to "deflect" rather than "reflect," we occupy ourselves (fill our minds) with whatever can be found among myriad options for entertainment. Whether through surfing the Internet, navigating hundreds of TV channels or engaging in chatty cell-phone conversations, our default programming seems to always favor "entertainment" or "inner attainment."

Our fear of being alone with ourselves, coupled with a penchant for seeking anchors in the external, or for seeking pseudo companionship, often compels us to remain in relationships that have long run their course. Yet, it is only when we return home (to the center of our being) to regroup our energies will we come to know that we are never alone. Operating in the default artist mode, there have been occasions when I was awake all night working on a particular project. Not having the luxury of sleeping-in the next day, the best I could do was to find 30 minutes or so that I could use just sitting or lying fully alert in quiet repose. I knew that if I could take a short while to center myself, I could regroup my energies and refresh myself. My approach was not that of a structured meditation. It did not include a mantra or any internal focus. I was just there, sitting quietly, being at peace. Thoughts came. I didn't entertain them. I let them come, do their dance and go. I just sat there, breathing in and breathing out. When I emerged from this place of stillness, my mind was more alert, my body felt refreshed and my flame was increased. In those times when you need an energy adjustment, take time (if only a few minutes) to dedicate to the practice of being still. Go into it without any particular aims or expectations. Just relax and allow yourself to be there. Lend yourself to the process, and allow the silence to minister to your needs.

Affirmation: In complete alignment with my best and highest self, I pull aside to go within, where the healing energy of silence ministers to the needs of my soul. I AM invigorated; I AM refreshed; I AM inspired.

*Reading for Value*

Another area of benefit - one where most of us lack sufficient commitment - is in reading. When it comes to seeking out and taking in information that will help us to better understand ourselves, face particular challenges from a more informed point of view or become more proficient at what we do, far too few are capitalizing on the benefits of the information age. Operating in old mindsets, that favor blind trust, the preference is to suffer through our dilemma uninformed, with hopes of stumbling upon a solution. Or we might just allow things to take their own course feeling they will work out on their own. There is an old adage that says "time changes things." And, while I agree that this is, essentially, true (in that change is inevitable), I am clear that what we do in the interim or with the "in-between time," contributes significantly to the nature and quality of the change. In other words, our consciously proactive, creative intent and actions not only influence the change, but have the power to dictate the outcome.

Making a commitment to seek out information that can help us to: do our jobs better, build better relationships, release ourselves from co-dependent tendencies and other unhealthy habits, or to understand and relieve unhealthy stress will go a long way toward harnessing the anxiety that often floods our lives and dampens our spirits. Another under-utilized asset at our disposal is information born of the experiences of others. While I am quite fond of the old adage that states: "Experience is the best teacher," I feel obliged to alert you that this principle does not come to us bearing the stipulation that it must be our own experience. In that our essence or the very core of our humanity is indelibly connected, the wisdom I gain from living is, by default, surrendered to the "cosmic pool of collective human understanding." Consequently, we have the right if not the obligation to draw from this pool as needed.

As do I, you might consider it a special blessing if someone passes your way to personally break off a piece of their wisdom for your personal edification. Allowing others to aid us in preparing for the changes we confront in life, constitutes this "gifting" as one of the least costly paths to accelerated growth. It is said that a daily commitment to thirty minutes of reading to better enhance your knowledge of your skill, trade or profession will make you better prepared than ninety-five percent (95%) of those in your field. I offer that the same applies to enhancing your ability to better understand, manage and master the opportunities and the challenges you confront in all areas of your life.

There is a biblical scripture (Hosea 4:6), that says we are destroyed due to a lack of knowledge. This axiom bears itself out in a statistic that says that only five percent (5%) of those who begin reading books actually finish them. This is a statistic that the word mediocrity doesn't begin to speak to. Yet, I hold out the hope that the advent of the information age, along with the increased popularity of the Internet and the convenient and accommodating nature of audio books will stimulate and facilitate a vigorous pursuit of life-enhancing information. I encourage you to pursue information that expands your consciousness, and better prepares you to navigate the changes and embrace the opportunities that lie ahead.

Utilize the vast resources at your disposal including the public library, your friend's book collection and the Internet. To balance out your reading you might want to incorporate casual material, such as fiction novels, comic strips and even a newspaper article or two. The key to managing the debilitating stress and unrest that often accompany change is to become informed and, therefore, self-determinate in those areas that generate stressful thoughts and feelings. This commitment can contribute

## Engaging the Spirit

much toward rekindling the inner fire that is a much needed commodity in your pursuit of Life Mastery.

Consider that there are basically two types of change - the change you initiate by your conscious or unconscious action, and change initiated in response to your conscious or unconscious resignation, passivity and indifference. It is your prerogative to experience the results of either. At various points in our lives, each of us has experienced either or both. In the way of encouraging you to be the conscious instigator of change, I leave you with this insight: The key to awakening the sleeping Genius within your soul is to offer to feed it passion, and to follow through in everything you do!

### *Summary*

- An attitude of disconnected indifference is not sufficient for lifting away the greasy remnants of a lifetime of mediocrity and discontent.

- A passion for doing all things well, in opposed to doing what it takes to "get by," is a key ingredient in the development of a Master Soul.

- We should remain alert and on guard concerning the messages we send to ourselves through our "self-talk."

- When used in conjunction, the two most powerful words in the universe, are "I" and "Am." Be mindful of the declarations that you choose to have follow these two powerful words.

- Sometimes it is necessary to take a methodical approach to over ride emotional downturns, and raise our enthusiasm.

- Daily, repeated affirmations provide a powerful method for renewing our minds - which is the key to transforming our lives.

- Maintaining and expressing an "attitude of gratitude" helps to ward-off the clouds of despair.

- Our bodies are the true "temple," and deserve greater attention than we give our physical dwellings and places of worship.

- Not only does physical exercise raise our level of physical energy, but it also contributes to our overall sense of well-being and at-one-ment.

- The practice of sitting still - free of any agenda or expectations - affords us the opportunity to regroup our energies and restore an overall sense of balance to our being.
- Taking the initiative to read thirty minutes of pertinent material per day will propel you to a level of preparedness exceeding that of 95 % of those in your field.
- The key to awakening the sleeping Genius within your soul is to offer to feed it passion, and to follow through in everything you do.

Engaging the Spirit

A Task: List a few things you do to boost your spirits during times when you feel challenged or overwhelmed. What additional practices might you consider adding to your process?

# Chapter 12

*Putting Your Dishes into the Water:*

*The Process of Surrender*

"*Submit Yourselves therefore to God.*"

- James 4:7

"*There are no more maps, no more creeds, no more philosophies. From here on in, the directions come straight from the Divine. The curriculum is being revealed millisecond by millisecond - invisibly, intuitively, spontaneously, lovingly. As one of Thomas Merton's monks has it, 'Go into your cell, and your cell will teach you everything there is to know.' Your cell - Yourself.*"

-Akashara Noor

All work, until now, has been geared toward arriving at this crucial point that I call surrender. Surrendering or submitting oneself to God does not mean that we abdicate responsibility for washing our dishes to someone or something else. It means that we have arrived at a point in consciousness where we're completely open to the higher understanding and guidance of the indwelling spirit. Though this guidance is always available to us and is certain and exact, our penchant for living external lives has deafened our receptivity to its voice. For most, it has become extremely difficult to distinguish the voice of intuitive counsel from the endless chatter of our subconscious minds. Yet, once our level of enthusiasm and passion rises to the point where we truly reverence life and are grateful for our role in it, we will begin to hear, more clearly from the voice of intuition or "the keeper of the key to the kingdom." Its purpose is to provide clear and specific instructions for the remainder of the dishwashing process. Our task is to slow down and become quiet enough to hear the its instruction. It is most important that when its call goes out, we stop everything and listen; for this is a major point of intersection - the point where mediocrity passes the baton to Mastery and Genius.

### The Tao of Dishwashing            Putting Your Dishes into the Water

The intelligence utilizing the voice of your inner being knows your issues and their order of priority. It will guide you as to which dishes to wash first - the glassware, silverware, pots, or pans. It will tell you which tools to use for which tasks, and guide you in determining which dishes require soaking and for how long. It will also let you know when to add hot water or change the water altogether. The key is in the listening - an area that provides many of us with our greatest challenge.

At this point of writing, a friend, Sharon Smith, related a poem she gleaned from "Living Positively, One Day at a Time," by Rev. Robert H. Schuler. In acknowledging Paul Laurence Dunbar as one of his favorite authors, he shared this poem, which has particular significance for the process of surrendering to God. Though this poem contains a clearly derogatory term that reflects a deeply racist human history, I commend Rev. Schuler for quoting the poem as Dunbar wrote it, and I share it in the same manner:

> "The Lord had a job for me, but I had so much to do I said, 'You get somebody else, Lord, or wait, till I get through.' I don't know how the Lord made out, but he seemed to get along. But I felt akinda sneekin' like I'd done the good Lord wrong. One day I needed the Lord, needed him right away! He never answered me at all, but I could hear him say down in my accusin' heart, 'Nigger I's got too much to do. You run along, or wait till I get through.' Now when the Lord's got a word for me, I never tries to shirk. I stop whatever Isa doin' to do the good Lord's work."

>                                                         - Paul Laurence Dunbar

With racial sensitivities and other concerns taken into consideration, while it may seem shocking to some, I use this poem to underscore the tendency to subvert the presence and power of spiritual guidance. As with Dunbar, we often do so by meandering down an alternative path. Most often, due to an inordinate sense of urgency, this is the path to which we've assigned the greatest priority. I hold no quarter when it comes to my commitment to emphasizing that, when the Lord of your spirit says, "I am ready to assist with your dishes," it's important for you to tune in, pipe down, and follow its directives.

# The Process of Surrender

## Cast Your Bread Upon the Waters

*There is something wonderfully healing about water. I remember the first time I saw the ocean. It wasn't that long ago, back in 1993. It was such an awe inspiring experience. It felt like coming home to me. I stood at its edge; simply taking in its song - a lyric, somehow familiar, rang true - spoke of voyages, journeys of long ago, into its breadth and depth, its blue. I stood there, pensive, like a sailor of old, who had somehow lost his way, finding himself again at port side, with strong desire to cast away.*

— Raja

"Commit thy works unto the Lord, and thy thoughts shall be established."

— Proverbs 16:3

Such is the powerful draw of spirit. We have each experienced times of casting our ships upon its waters and utilizing its powerful and rhythmic flow to transport us to the ports of our desire. It is the memory of these times that calls us back to the ocean of our unlimited connectedness with our highest nature. This is the place of holy communion and sweet surrender. Though longing for the peace and solace that connectedness with the Divine promises, for many, the concept of surrendering to anything suggests a level of vulnerability that beckons resistance. Quite often that resistance rises to the level of self-sabotage. By virtue of a prevailing societal mindset that glorifies war, and lauds "winner-take-all" competition, our altered egos are programmed to feast on any opportunity to subdue and conquer. Being programmed in such a way, we are geared to never surrender without a fight.

Evidence of this surfaced a few years ago while I attended a gathering of a small group. During part of the meeting, before a particular presentation, a standard affirmation was repeated several times. Included in the affirmation was the line: "I surrender lack." Also attending was a brother new to Atlanta from Los Angeles, who would not repeat that portion of the affirmation. He actually tried and admitted experiencing a noticeable degree of discomfort repeating the words, "I surrender." He shared with the group that he seemed to have a psychological block that prohibited him from entertaining the idea of surrendering to anything, on any level for any reason. It seems that a life of struggling to accomplish his ends and manifest his desires had created within him a resolve that left no room for surrender. As a result, he could not bring himself to say the words, "I surrender." He is not alone. The evidence of our own resistance may manifest in more subtle or more aggressive ways. Yet, the fact remains that it's common human drama to wrestle, in some way, with the concept of surrendering. At a minimum, it's a common experience to grapple with the dilemma of when to "hold on" or "let go," as well as when to "make things happen" versus "allow things to happen." This often ceaseless tug of war within our minds is largely responsible for the inordinate amount of time and struggle involved in manifesting our dreams.

When given charge of plotting the course for our lives, our altered-ego (fragmented idea of Self) is accustomed to working alone and at mental and emotional center stage. As a result, it has become so isolated and overblown that we ignore the fact that the event we are staging (life in human form in pursuit of life purpose) is a process as well as a "team sport." I'm sure we all agree that the phenomenon that we call time appears to have sped up to the extent that the idea of "losing track of time" has taken on new meaning. As the pace of our lives accelerates, so does the sense that there are more things to do than we have time for. As a result, our preference is that events (particularly new events) arrive in our lives highly processed and in need of little or no special care. In lieu of the quick fix, this quickening of our pace has us in a mode where we tend to shy away from processes, particularly processes that we can't manage and move along at a pace the suits us. The stress associated with the notion that time has sped up and that we are racing against time has within it the potential to cause us to move at a pace that outstrips our help. The fact is that there is aid and assistance that can be duly afforded by other members of our team...aid and assistance that are imperative to the successful outcome of our endeavor.

As one charged with discovering, developing and leaning on the strength of my individual talents and abilities, I know what it's like to suffer an aversion to team efforts. Yet, I am clear that the way of the "lone ranger" had its season and its intent - an understanding that has become integrated into my being. At this point of the journey, my charge is to surrender the use of my acquired talents and abilities in concert with a larger vision that encompasses our collective humanity.

# The Process of Surrender

Any observer of the nature of team sports will attest that the team with the "hot shot superstar" with plenty of individual talent but no concept of team play never wins a championship. The same is so with us when our altered ego is "running its game." We fail to realize that we have help and, therefore, fail to realize our ultimate objective - to champion our life. Confused or deceived about the true nature of power, and accustomed to deferring to the mind as the seat of Genius and creativity, we are prone to self-service. Thus, rarely are we in position to receive and follow through on the inspiration and spiritual guidance that come our way. Just like the "hot shot superstar" who hardly ever passes the ball, we often find ourselves in no position to receive (in return) the pinpoint pass that would meet us at our favorite spot on the floor, were we to learn to play the team game.

Utilizing this basketball team analogy, all players have differing degrees of all the skills required to play the game. But, more important, they all have roles. Though their roles are critical, not all players touch the ball on every play. Some may be charged with setting a pick or screen clear critical space for the eventual scorer. Another player (quite often the best scorer) may serve as a decoy who draws the attention of multiple defenders, in order to divert attention from the intended scorer. Given this idea of utilizing the benefits of a "team approach" to unfold your path to mastery, understand that each aspect of your being plays a specific role. Spirit, as orchestrator, coach, floor general, or "point guard" has the role of creating the idea, (in-spir-ation), sending this inspiration to the mind, and coordinating your mind, body, and emotional natures to do those things necessary to bring the idea to fruition. The intellect assumes the role of receiving an idea, assessing its possibilities and organizing the mental construct or plan for the execution of the idea. Likewise, our emotions have the role of supplying the energies of faith, joy, vigor and passion, which fuel the fire that drives the idea. Our physical bodies are the vehicle through which the idea is executed and made manifest.

Interestingly enough, resting beneath it all, providing the impetus to "enter the game in the first place," is a healthy, properly integrated ego. Here's how it works. Understanding that the play is coming its way, your mind (or intellect) has the task of going through whatever moves are necessary to "get itself open" and in position to receive the ball, so that it can pass it on to the body for the shot. But, before that shot can be taken, your emotional nature has the role of "setting screens," so that undermining emotions (defenders) are filtered out, and don't show up to interfere or "block the shot." If the shot is missed or a pass goes awry, all players are required to retain possession by scrambling for the loose ball. When the other team (altered-ego) is on the offensive, rather than standing passively by while it scores a lay up, slam dunk or hits an uncontested three-pointer, each player is also required to play defense. If the given play is executed as designed, the result is unstoppable brilliance and magnificence that manifests through the deeds done in the body. Having defined a suitable objective, the primary quality distinguishing the Genius from the average individual lies in his or her ability to surrender the rule of ego and allow higher guidance to direct his or her creative process. Those who understand this truth and align with it bring forth dynamic works that uplift themselves, their families, communities, and humanity. Those who don't create reasonable facsimiles but, invariably, leave something on the table.

The most wonderful benefits I've gained in life are the tributes paid by those who attest that their lives have been significantly changed through their brief encounters or personal relationships with me. Some attribute those changes to the message and energy of my music and written material. Others credit my unalterable alignment with my message. Given the many years of hardship, challenge and struggle required to strike a balance among the many aspects of my being and, thereby, unfold my destiny, this testament - of an enhanced human life - is the much sought after and highly valued fruit of my life tree. It is also a significant step toward the ultimate realization of my heart's desire. What about you? This ability to emanate an energy which brings forth the best from within yourself and others is your birthright. Claim it, and use it!

To aid you in ensuring that your ego is not grandstanding and usurping the power inherent in the team effort that is the rightful process for your life energies, consider this: There is a "touchstone" or model of fighting spirit, deeply embedded within the human psyche. It rests at the center of our Kingdom, and bears responsibility for maintaining the vitality of the flame of our life-purpose and heart's desire. Composed of the energies of clear intent, pinpoint focus, a wiling mind, and a receptive and adaptive spirit, Its job is to make sure that we never quit - that we continue our quest for Self-Mastery. It is from this model that an illegitimate copy has been forged and established at the center of the potentially bereft kingdoms of intellect and personality. In order to align with this resident Genius and be counted among the Masters, we must properly align these energies and surrender them back to the Source. This process of surrender will signal our souls to denounce the ill-advised rule of altered-ego and its counterfeit domain. The essence of life mastery is contained within our ability to reverse the overthrow. We can do so through mastering this distinction and, thereby, re-establishing rightful rule of the kingdom.

## *Summary*

- There is an inherent aspect of our being that resists the notion of surrendering to anything; under any circumstances.

- The proper channeling of this "spirit of determination" will insure the ultimate success of our desires.

- The act of "surrendering to higher wisdom" does not mean that we abdicate our responsibility for taking constructive action.

- The altered ego, with its false sense of self-sufficiency, channels its energy through an intellectual and egocentric approach to creativity. This is a disjointed approach, which, ultimately "leaves something on the table."

- The ability to receive guidance, inspiration, and direction from a source higher than that of intellectual reasoning, is a defining characteristic of true Genius.

- Casting the ships of our hopes, dreams, and aspirations upon the sea of spiritual guidance will yield, seemingly, miraculous results.

A Task: In what ways has your ego resisted surrendering to the guidance of your spirit? What experiences or thought processes can you identify as the basis for this resistance?

Affirmation: "I return to the center of my being where the fire of life purpose fuels my efforts. I reject the rule of altered ego, and surrender to the higher wisdom and guidance of the true keeper of my kingdom flame."

# Chapter 13

*Soaking Your Dishes: The Process of Meditation*

*"Come unto me all ye who labor and are heavy laden, and I will give you rest."*

- Matthew 11:28

Putting your dishes into the water required that you release and cast away the restrictive shackles of ego-centered or "limited self" control. Now it's time to allow the cosmically attuned rhythms of your inner ocean to serenade you with your unique and dynamic song. This process can only be engaged by pulling aside into a quiet place…into the space of meditation.

While it has long remained commonplace for us to wander through life hoping to stumble upon some idea of divine intent for our lives, we are living in an age when it is our destiny to be clear about our purpose. The time has come to explode through old paradigms, and establish new criteria as baselines for every aspect of our existence. The nature of human life is that we are afforded a broad spectrum of opportunity to engage experience that will aid in expanding our awareness of our inner truth. Yet, before descending the ladder to embark the earth plane, as spiritual beings, operating in realms beyond physical perception, we chose to narrow our intent to focus on specific areas of growth. Commitments to becoming consciously aware of our soul's intent, and making a deliberate effort to master these areas of growth and unfoldment are the keys to Life Mastery and Genius. They also provide a clear path to the gate to our Kingdom..

At the seat of the soul rests what I refer to as the "major life lessons" (or remembrances). These are specific aspects of Being that each of us has come to awaken and reinforce. This informational deposit represents the primary area(s) where we have come to focus our "re-membering," or the rejoining of parts of ourselves that have become dismembered and scattered or neglected and abandoned. It's important to note that, along with our personal growth objectives, each of us has a contribution to make to the greater vision of an expanded, more enlightened humanity. Though some have chosen to take on more visible or prominent roles, we are each called to make a personal and unique entry in the cosmic journal. This is the great book into which the collective urge to expand and beautify the landscape of human potential is inscribed. This is an incessant call that resonates from the Spirit of Creation into each of our hearts. Whether we rise to the occasion to be counted among those whose humanity makes an indelible impact upon the lives of others depends on whether we choose to answer the call. In order to effectively participate, we would do well to connect with insight into what contribution we might best make. This information is readily available within your heart of hearts. It can also be validated by you, through accessing information that is readily available in the world.

I've had many occasions to consult with individuals about their particular life lessons and the assignments they have taken on during this critical phase in our evolutionary process. In setting the stage for our discoveries, I've found it useful to draw a parallel between the pursuit of our soul's intent and the quest to obtain a Master's Degree at an institution of higher learning. I explained the process in this fashion: Chances are that when we decide to enroll in college, we have a pretty clear idea about the area of discipline we'll pursue. From the onset, we may be clear and intentional about moving through undergraduate school to the post graduate level, in pursuit of a Master's Degree in say, Business Administration. This clear intentionality is synonymous with our soul's intent to "master" a particular aspect of humanity. For example, this could pertain to "Being self-assertive and developing and maintaining the strength of ones' convictions." The particular intent is personal and specific to you and me. When we become intentional about gaining clarity around our soul's objectives, we can access information as particular as that which would equate to "courses of study," as well as particular "class schedules and syllabus content."

The normal modality for the evolving soul is comparable to a "work/study program," where an agreement is struck to exchange personal effort, knowledge and other energy forms in service to the institution that affords us entry. The truly delightful thing about this mutually beneficial

## The Process of Meditation

"work/study" arrangement is that we come to the task fully qualified to be acknowledged and employed as instructors. In fact, it is my belief that, at this point in our evolution, we each hold Master's degrees in one if not several significant areas of human understanding. Most often, we don't consciously see this reality as it plays out in our life experience. Yet, rather than being regulated to a job in the bookstore or cafeteria, our opportunity is to stand tall and share our inherent knowing, as instructors. So, while in possession of at least one Master's degree, we enroll the earth plane in pursuit of another. When we are operating in accord with life to fulfill our soul's contract, this is my assessment of the ideal way our process is intended to unfold.

The reality is that it's rare to find someone who possesses the level of clarity that would place them squarely on pace with their soul's agenda. Instead, it's more common to find that we've enrolled in college with the intent of pursuing one area of mastery only to have our direction altered by some external set of circumstances. Simply stated, these alternative directives flow from the command center of the kingdom of altered-ego. Even so, after getting into the particulars with various individuals, I've found that the majority are aware, at least to the extent of being able to recognize their truth when they hear it. We are then able to use this truth to identify patterns in their lives that correlate with the information we are sharing. Some respond with "Wow! So that's why I felt so strongly about following this particular course of study," or "Yes, that's something that has been a challenge for me. Becoming aware of it's source will certainly help me to make headway toward mastering it."

I've also encountered those who, despite myriad repeated experiences presented for their enlightenment, chose to remain hidden, even to themselves. Holding fast to convention, they chose to anchor themselves at a level of consciousness that sprouts such declarations as: "If God wanted us to fly, he would have given us wings!" or "If it ain't in the Bible, I ain't gonna believe it!" Such resistance to broadening our perception and embracing change has a significant part of the populace afraid to learn the use of a computer, utilize ATM machines or visit the library to surf the web. Fearing a threat to our coveted sense of ego-based security (as established through religion, cultural indoctrination or otherwise), the prospect of venturing outside well-established boundaries is nill. Unsure of what we might discover if we pull the back the blinds and allow sunlight to warm and illumine our consciousness, rather than embrace its inherent possibility for enriching our lives we choose to shrink in the face of a challenging new opportunity. Our hope is that by unplugging the phone that connects us to inner voices prompting us toward change, we can avoid answering the call to rise, explore and expand the kingdom. Consequently, though enrolled on a planet that is in the midst of a bustling information revolution, we ultimately render ourselves numb, dumb, clueless, and ill-prepared for change. This way of being in the world creates blockages to new insight and is co-sponsor of our penchant for concluding that - God and, thus life, works in ways that are far too mysterious for us to understand. So, we employ an inordinate sense of surrender - trusting things will, of their own accord, work to our benefit.

We each have had the experience of soaking in a hot bath, and allowing the water, soap, bath oils, Epsom salts, or other ingredients to rejuvenate our bodies. The process of meditation is similar, in that it opens, cleans and invigorates our spiritual pores. The soaking process soothes the aching muscles of a consciousness struggling to make sense of the seemingly random nature of life circumstance. Through the process of meditation (soaking your dishes), your spiritual guidance will expose those baked-on, crusty areas in your consciousness that create impediments to your growth. With your consent, it will begin to gently plow beneath them, loosening their grip, and dissolving them into nothingness. This is a much-needed process for clearing the path for establishing a broader foundation of possibilities within your thinking. With this newly found liberty, you can begin to seek, in earnest, for the part you can play in the unfolding of a newly emerging world. Whether you utilize music, focus your attention on a particular thought, challenge or desire or just sit with an attentive ear, the opportunity is to have a space to relax, soak up the healing energy of divine guidance and have built-up layers of illusion peeled away.

*Uprooting Deeply-seated Deposits of Mis-identity*

*"I decided I had too much to lose, so I made up in my mind to clear the way. I'm so delighted to know that I can choose to linger in the dark or face a brand new day, so I'm changing."*

- The Voices of Change - Raja

## The Process of Meditation

After soaking awhile, the gentle caress of the waves of your inner ocean will begin to loosen layer upon layer of baked on mis-identity. These needless layers are synonymous with the "etcetera," or the foundation and makeup of the "Earth Theater Community." As you release your attachment to your ego identities, a new perspective on your potential emerges from beyond the facades of race, color, gender, religious affiliation, and economic and social status. At the shear delight of getting to the truth of who you are, your joy, passion and enthusiasm elevate the temperature of the water, and prompt even deeper levels of relaxation, self-discovery and release. Your mind begins to expand, as it releases many of its limited concepts about the nature of reality. You may begin to experience a softening sensation in the area of your heart, as your latent, time-hardened beliefs concerning your racial superiority or inferiority begin to loosen, break up, and dissolve. There - far beneath the costume layers of hair and skin - you will come face-to-face with a spiritual being akin to all others, created in the image and likeness of God.

While quietly contemplating your true purpose, attention may be drawn to your lust for the physical and sensual pleasures of this world - the things that money and worldly power so easily avail. As you allow the travel log of your life to unfold before your inner eyes, it reveals a pattern of over-indulging the physical appetites to the neglect of your overall well-being. You may discover that your tendency to overindulge the use of food, alcohol, tobacco, sex, and drugs stems from the sense that there is something lacking in your life. There may exist a sense that this void may never be filled. It may be revealed that your penchant for excess is a mechanism you devised in an attempt to escape a sense of hopelessness and insufficiency. It may also be your way of providing yourself a default mode of nurturing and self-fulfillment. In this safe and nurturing environment of complete self-surrender, you are encouraged to peer beyond these illusions to glimpse the "Transcendental Self." This is the real you, fully poised and endowed with unlimited potential and the absolute power of self-determination. Before the processes of dissolution and disillusion can begin, you are prompted to "choose this day whom you will serve." The choices are simple - The limited self, with pursuit of its selfish and short term pleasures and penchant for undermining your pursuit of Life-Mastery; or the Transcendental Self - the fully liberated, highly motivated heir and rightful ruler of the kingdom.

As this highly personal and intimate process unfolds, many will have it revealed that - through jealousy, possessiveness and a desire to control the activities and restrict the freedom of others, you, yourself, have become bound. You will see that your sense of having limited opportunities to advance beyond a certain level in life is directly related to the lack of liberty you afford others who are under your influence. Through allowing yourself to be liberated from a hidden sense of insecurity and fear of loss, you immediately expand the sphere of your potential, influence and opportunity. In this moment of complete clarity, surrender and acceptance, you release the idea that you are not loved and respected. You surrender the notion that, in order for things to go your way, you must rule over your relationships with an iron fist. As this aspect of your persona gives way to the more loving, caring and accepting being that you choose to be, as they flow into the space you have provided in your heart, allow yourself to receive the energies of self-love, self-acceptance and cooperation.

Could it be that you are an old soul on the final leg of a long journey home? That being so, as you work to complete your theater schedule and release your attachment to the world of physicality, your task is to wear a myriad of costumes and play a plethora of roles? Can you see any areas where the tendency to hold on to comfortable and familiar roles and conditions has created stagnation in your life? Or, though you desperately long for things to remain the same, are you having the experience of people, conditions and things constantly and painfully exiting your life? Among the treasures unearthed during these priceless moments of reflection and contemplation, may come the understanding that your task is to allow experiences to come and go in your life, while releasing your tendency to grip too tightly and hold on for too long. Allow your inner guidance to reveal the challenges that continue to hold you within their grip, and guide you through the process of their detachment and release.

By sitting in quiet expectancy, this crucial information, or that which is "formed within," will begin to surface from beneath the multifarious layers of illusion and false indoctrination. This information, which is specific to you and your journey, is stored within the library of your own inner knowing. It can be retrieved "by you," when you commit to soaking your dishes or retreating to the space of mediation and contemplation.

## The Process of Meditation

There is a biblical saying which states: "Many are called, but few are chosen." In my assessment, that which distinguishes the called from the chosen is the response to the call. In that the chosen "chose" to answer the call when it came, they chose to be chosen. How about you? Are you prepared to surrender to the guidance of your inner knowing, and allow it to assist you with mending those aspects of being that have become dismembered through your disassociation? If this is your true desire, "Ask, and it shall be given. As you seek, you shall find."

### *Summary*

- As spiritual beings engaging a quest for life mastery, we choose to embark a path that will unfold opportunities to learn life particular life lessons.

- An inner (soul) awareness of these challenges creates opportunities that enable us to grow through them.

- Taking time to meditate upon the recurring themes of our lives from a non-judgmental point of view - will cause the layers of illusion to fall away, enabling us to grasp the opportunities these challenges afford.

- Our tendency toward "unplugging the phone" though seeking refuge in the outside world, is responsible for our missing the call to journey within to engage a deeper understanding of our reason for being.

- Gaining conscious awareness of these challenges (through available information) jump-starts our ability to overcome them, and accelerates our ascent into Life-Mastery.

- The difference between the "called" and the "chosen" is that the chosen "chose" to answer the call.

A Task: Take time to examine your consciousness for "sticking points" - those recurring themes that seem to show up - with "fists flailing" - in key areas of your life. Are you too gullible and, thus, willing to believe whatever others tell you? Under the guise of a "realist," are you generally insensitive to the thoughts, feelings and needs of others? Whether wealthy or presumed poor, do you live with the fear of an inability to properly handle money, and are learning to free yourself from the grasp of a poverty consciousness? Are there latent hints of racial insensitivity and/or cultural bias and fear hiding beneath your facade of religious or civic good will?"

Affirmation: "I surrender to the guidance of infinite internal wisdom, knowledge and understanding. I am led to the library of my own self-knowing, where, from a book of my own authorship, I review the intimate details of my life lessons or reason for being."

# Chapter 14

## Washing Your Dishes: The Practical Application of Principle

*"Let every man prove his own work, and then shall he have rejoicing in himself alone, and not in another. For every man shall bear his own burden."*

- Galatians 6:4-5

As is the case with most ventures, the key to a successful end lies, primarily, in proper preparation. If you've followed and benefited from the steps of the dishwashing process thus far, you should be gaining clarity about the nature of your particular stack of dishes. This knowledge relates to the true nature and condition of your soul, and the spots and blemishes that impede you from shining. You are also prepared to begin washing away these impediments. Having properly engaged the meditative process, you've opened yourself to receive intimate knowledge and heightened awareness into the nature of your major life lessons. You have also availed yourself to guidance as to how to proceed with mastering them. Now it's time to utilize the information by putting your heart, mind, spirit, and hands to work. All aspects of being are brought to bear in the unified task of purging your soul of the impurities that have bound you to mediocrity.

It's important to note that even though your washing environment may lie within the confines of structured religion, with its attendant leadership, no one can wash your dishes for you. It's not enough to put yourself in the position to gain information and insight. It's mandatory that you "bear your own burden," through making practical, hands-on application of the information and tools made available to you.

### Know Your Patterns

An inscription over the gate of the Oracle at Delphi, Greece (circa 6 B.C.) admonished all comers to: "Know Thyself." In preparing to wash away the dross of illusion from your unique set of dishes, it is a good idea to make an assessment of the shape, pattern and other characteristics of each item - to connect with each and become familiar with any areas that may prove difficult to access. In examining your life, you will discover that your major lessons - though seemingly inaccessible and hidden from the casual glance - have been present all along - revealing themselves in the dominant patterns of your life. Theoretically, you might examine the rims of jars and glasses, the lips of pots, pans, skillets and lids, the intricate patterns of glass stemware, and the handles of cutlery and silverware.

Back in 1986, three years removed from the pulpit, and many years into literally yearning for clarity about the path of my destiny, I hit bottom. I was doing one of my entrepreneurial things (a used car lot in Forest Park, Georgia) - a venture I entered into with my father. We had no money to speak of, but we were risk-takers with quite a history of success at making something out of nothing. As car salesmen working together at a local Buick dealership, we were hailed as "the greatest one-two-punch the local car business had ever seen." There was a particular month (April 1978) when we sold fifty-nine cars between us. So, in undertaking this new venture, though we had no money to speak of, we felt that procuring and selling twenty to twenty- five cars together in our own enterprise would be a snap. So, we set out to make a success of our endeavor.

This was a period of major upheaval in my life, thus this venture proved to be an important opportunity for mastering emotional self-control. I was at the point of no return where my marriage was concerned, and feeling miserable about not being with my children. Consequently, I sparred, daily, with the ghosts of a religious indoctrination that programmed my mind to believe that my current life path was a fast track to hell. There were other aspects of my life that were also turned upside down. So, it was good for me to have something creative, though difficult, to focus on and pour my energy into. We found this great, corner lot on Jonesboro road (in Forest Park, Georgia), and established "I-Deal Cars." While my father continued to work at another dealership, the responsibility for setting up and running the business fell to me. Part of his decision to continue at his job was based on his ability to access trade-ins that we could purchase for our inventory. I had started several businesses in the past (one of them with my father) and, despite the highly

## The Practical Application of Principle

unpleasant nature of our past experience, I embraced this enterprise as an opportunity to both reconcile the past and invoke as a creative outlet for my litany of skills. I went about getting a dealer's license and insurance, establishing a bank account, getting the utilities turned on, repairing, cleaning and painting the building, and appraising, reconditioning, pricing, selling, and writing finance contracts on the cars we sold.

From the start, we literally began performing miracles. Through his association with the used car manager, my dad supplied our lot with inexpensive trade-ins that sold quickly. In lieu of a cash sale, our policy was to - at a minimum - secure all hard costs invested in the vehicle though a down payment. Then, we would carry a note for payments that would be paid on a weekly basis. Things went along well for a few months until an old familiar pattern of misappropriation was exposed and our operations were brought to a halt. Major problems arose when the dealership owner (whom he met through me and who was a friend of mine) came by the lot to inform me that my father had received cars from his lot that he had not paid him for. In fact, the used car manager and not he had authorized the arrangement.

At the root of the problem was the fact that a few of the cars in question were cars I had sold and given him the money to pay for. Well, I was livid. Not only was I angry and disappointed with my father, but I was angry with myself for allowing his practice of either coming to get or sending for the money generated for a sale, rather than allowing the funds to flow through our business account. At the root of my anger was the fact that, since a similar pattern of deception has surfaced years earlier when we joined forces in another endeavor, I knew better than to conduct business that way.

Though I didn't particularly care for the way they unfolded, at that time I was clear that the primary significance of these events was to provide an opportunity for me to confront a pattern evident in both my father's behavior and mine. In as calm a fashion as I could, I took this matter up with my father who made no apologies for his doings. In fact, my complaint was checked by a level of audacity that was so dismissive that I literally reeled back on my heels. He ranted, effusively, about how he was going to run this business any way he chose, and there wasn't a damn thing I could do about it! The bottom line, for him, was that if I didn't like it, I could move on, and he would get someone else to run "his business." I stood there teetering on the brink of crossing that proverbial line that divides dearly beloved from mortal enemy. In that moment, I stood poised, if need be, to engage him in a "beat down." I told him that he might indeed run his business any way he chose, but he wasn't going to do it at that location or under the name "I-Deal Cars!" And, for very good reasons, on that day, our paths parted. I stayed - he left.

Standing up to my father in this way marked a significant turning point for me. Since childhood, I harbored deep sensitivities concerning him. As a small child, I longed for his presence, and wrestled with what his not being there for me said about my value to him. During my teen years, on the few occasions that I visited him in Detroit, I recall being reduced to tears whenever he would chastise, criticize or say anything harsh to me. By standing up to him, on this and other occasions that arose, I've been able to strengthen my own sense of identity, and work through all issues that plagued me concerning him. One of those issues centered around my stepfather's insistence that, just like my father, I would never amount to anything. Well, the fact is that I did not see my father in such lowly terms at all. In fact, though I saw him rarely, I was aware of quite a bit of his nature as well as his talents, abilities and accomplishments. He had a wonderful singing voice that he put on display through traveling the club circuit. He seemed to travel a regular circuit that included Buffalo, New York and Toronto, Canada. He also had an indomitable entrepreneurial spirit and a kind, humanitarian heart. These were traits that I saw and admired, as well as identified in myself.

Yet, with my stepfather's idea haunting the recesses of my subconscious, it became important for me to distinguish myself from my father. It became indelibly clear that I must disassociate myself from what I perceived as the "negative aspects of his being." The reason I would cower whenever he displayed behaviors that were intemperate or that seemed abusive is that, in an effort to deal with the shadows that haunted me concerning our "sameness," my delicate sense of self shuttered at the thought that I could be as insensitive as he seemed to be. I also recoiled at the thought that I could do some of the things he did...things that I considered unconscionable. As painful as it was, at certain levels, our encounter at I-Deal Cars afforded me an opportunity to clearly define myself in relationship to my father.

# The Practical Application of Principle

Despite the aforementioned challenges, the effort that I put into establishing and maintaining I-Deal Cars lit a fire within me that I was unwilling to have snuffed out. Having had two similar businesses fizzle (Expert Auto Cleaning and S&L Home Improvement), I dreamed of a third opportunity to make a successful go of it. Thus, I was determined to hold that vision and "will" I-Deal Cars into a successful endeavor. So, there I remained with the task of parlaying an inventory of two cars into an enterprise that would carry the weight of approximately three-thousand dollars worth of monthly overhead. That was in addition to my personal and family financial responsibilities. Some cash flow had been established by virtue of our "buy here-pay here" financing program, but even that flow dried up, as I spent more time tracking down payments than anything else. Though my hopes remained high, with no inventory to reinvigorate the cash flow, time was rapidly winding down.

## At "Whit's End"

I spent Thanksgiving Day, 1986, sitting alone at the office, literally contemplating whether to "do or die." Despite dreadful conditions (two cars on the lot - one of them running), with ultimate hopes of purchasing the property, I was determined to maintain possession of that property. Despite conditions that would thwart the hopes of any reasonable person, this dream kept my creative juices flowing at an all time high. During that time, though I had no idea where the next opportunities lie, I was diligently applying the principles I share in this book. While dog paddling in the midst of a dark and tumultuous sea of circumstance a piece of "driftwood" came floating by. To keep the possibility of success alive, the idea came to utilize the lot for selling Christmas trees. I immediately seized upon the inspiration. I felt that I could sell enough trees to afford me the money to make it into the new year, when things were bound to improve. There was only one problem: I had no money to stock the lot with trees. But that would not stop me. I was determined that no matter how waterlogged this piece of driftwood, I would convert it into kindlin'! I sat quietly listening for ideas, and came up with an alternate method for acquiring my new inventory.

I searched the phone book and made connection with a wholesaler who was doing business at the Georgia Farmer's Market. He agreed to supply me with one hundred trees, with the agreement that I would pay him after I sold the trees. What a blessing! With deep gratitude, I danced, rejoiced and thanked the Creator for this breakthrough. This was just the sign I needed to reinforce my belief that my destiny was tied to this venture...that I would, ultimately, end up with this property and a well-stock inventory of nice used cars. At last, after picking up the trees, squaring the bottoms, making stands, and displaying them on the lot, I had inventory! Well, in spite of my relentless hope and perseverance, and the practice of holding watch over them, the end result was the loss of twenty-four trees to thieves. Need I say that this made for a very, very less than merry Christmas? After deducting the cost of one hundred trees and the extra lighting and material that went into building the stands and signs, I barely broke even and almost broke down. With no understanding of how what I felt "God was doing to insure my breakthrough" had clearly served to add momentum to my seemingly imminent demise, I fell into a state of depression. I didn't understand. I had worked hard, exercised faith, vision and integrity, prayed without ceasing, exercised patience, perseverance and creativity, yet, I had "failed."

## A "Cry in the Wilderness"

*"There are times when my path through life seems like scaling a mountain, and I wonder how in the world would I make the climb. Through the clouds of fear I see no sunlight shining. With no relief in sight, I feel that I'm losing my mind. Deep down inside, I know there's a place where I can go, where the troubles of this world can't hold me bound...where I am free to be the transcendental me; no limitations, no frustrations, no dark clouds."*

- Fly Away - Raja

Spending the last few days of the year in relative isolation, I poured out my soul, literally wailing in grief. Three days out from my thirty-third birthday, I was reduced to petitioning heaven for some glint of hope - for any reason to continue living. My world had fallen apart and, absent the resolve to attempt holding the pieces together any longer, I committed to taking my life. While sitting there in that office with a bottle of Cognac in one hand and a 9mm semiautomatic Uzi in the other, though grief-stricken, destitute and with "one or two sheets in the wind," after crying out for days, I heard, from the depths of my seemingly threadbare soul, a voice that I'll simply refer to as God. This is what it said - "You have forgotten what you know of me and have listened to men. Now, you perish. Forget everything you think you know of me. Lend me your ear and

## The Practical Application of Principle

I will cause you to remember who I AM, and who you are in me." For the sake of expediency, I will say that I was directed to go to the bookstore, of all places - and I did so, that very day. Having no idea what book or books to look for, I simply "showed up" and allowed myself to be directed to whatever books they were. Bear in mind that, by virtue of my religious indoctrination, the only book considered to have any value for spiritual growth was the Bible, and I already had one of those. So I had no clue. But my Inner Guide did. After browsing the store for a short while, I was drawn to two books that demanded my attention. I purchased them, headed back, and began reading as soon as I returned to the office. The first was "Psycho Cybernetics," by Maxwell Maltz, and the second, 'Think and Grow Rich," by Napoleon Hill. Though I never followed through, both were books a minister friend (Reverend Jim Higginbottom) encouraged me to read sixteen years earlier.

The information in these books sparked a resurgence of hope within my spirit, and started me on an unrelenting quest for self-knowledge and human understanding that unfolded the path to my destiny. A short time thereafter - despite the added hope these books engendered - I concluded that I was "all in." I had received many benefits including enhanced communication skills, a heightened exercise in persistence, renewed faith, and a breakthrough in the areas that challenged concerning my father. I resigned to accepting that to "deal cars" was not my destiny. I released any further expectations and moved on.

*"Looking back on "used to be," some buried treasure I might find, while sifting through my faded memories. But I must gather up the strength to leave what's history behind, I hear the call of destiny. So, I AM Changing."*

The Voices of Change (Are Calling Out My Name) - Raja

### Back on Track

My own process of self-discovery, which has incorporated all aspects and many slants on what I call "The Tao of Dishwashing," has afforded me clarity about my particular "set of dishes" or Life Lessons. They encompass the very things that have caused me the greatest challenge over the course of my life. Simply stated they are - Learning to "detach" and let go of old belief systems and assignments that kept me from moving forward to embrace new opportunities, and to allow things to come and go in my life, with no need to possess, control or hold onto them. I found that, like the man who walked the same street and fell into the same hole on three different occasions, there were times when I held onto and continued with a thing beyond the point where it benefited my soul and the souls of others. In understanding that I have come into the world to embrace a wide spectrum of experience, it is for me to enjoy them, learn from them, contribute to them, and to release them, and move on. It is my lot to know when to cease, desist and "take a different road." Becoming consciously aware of this has helped me to see the events of my life from a clearer perspective, and to identify the hidden cracks and crevices where deposits and residue of these tendencies might yet be found.

While preparing to wash your particular stack of dishes, it's important to utilize the guidance you received while in the meditative or soaking state. It's beneficial to have a clear methodical approach, and to maintain a sense of priority or working order. You may choose to handle the plates, china, glasses, stemware, and other emotionally sensitive fragile-ware first. Or you may opt for tackling the more physically challenging tasks, synonymous with burnt spaghetti pots and baked-on macaroni dishes. Go with the guidance of your Spirit. Filter each of your issues (each intimate detail, characteristic and quality) through the vision you glimpsed of yourself fully actualized. Utilizing whatever tools you find necessary, begin to wash each dish with this vision of wholeness in mind. You may rediscover tools that have been at your disposal for twenty years that you set aside without ever putting them to use. Don't hesitate to pull them out and use them. Make sure that you are not merely glancing over the surfaces. Get your finger-guided dishcloth on each spot and in every crevice, crack and corner. Though you may feel you have done a thorough job, it may benefit you to run your fingers over the object to reinspect it. You may discover something that requires the utilization of your fingernail or a scraper or scrub pad to remove it. Whatever it takes, be thorough and passionate! Connect with the task. This is the level of conscious awareness that you must commit to bringing into practice in everything you do. Remember that in this process of moving from mediocrity to Mastery, all of your energies must align.

> *"Remember you cannot abandon what you do not know. To go beyond yourself, you must know yourself."*
>
> -Sri Nisargadatta Majaraj

# The Practical Application of Principle

## *Summary*

- Know your patterns.
- When properly applied, knowledge is power.
- Self-knowledge will allow you to work intelligently at releasing undermining tendencies and uprooting hidden pockets of false identity.
- The process of recovering your soul could spur some sense of crisis in your life.
- The growth that your Soul desires may, ultimately, require that you release every bit of what you have come to intellectually and emotionally accept as your "truth."
- In allowing your guidance to flow from the center of your being, your life perspective will become enhanced. It is then that you will begin to connect with the truth and value that is resident within you and all things.
- All of your energies must align in the process of moving from mediocrity to Mastery.

A Task: What particular area(s) of your life have generated the most resistance and provided you with your greatest challenge(s)? Describe the particulars of the challenge(s) in terms that might identify it as a "life lesson." What steps are you taking toward mastering this challenge(s)?

Affirmation: "I am in tune with the intimate details of my life lessons (those things which I am working to remember). As I lovingly scour my soul, I remove all resistance to growth, and through practical application, I allow all tools and processes to work to my benefit."

# Chapter 15

Rinsing Your Dishes: The Final Clearing

*"Let every soul be subject to the higher powers. For there is no power but of God: the powers that be are ordained of God."*

-Romans 13:1

Having treated each of your dishes to a thorough washing, it's time for them to undergo the final examination. As with each prior process, the rinsing stage or what I call the "final clearing" must be engaged with a high level of passion and positive expectancy. It requires hot water and a keen, spirit-directed eye, or what we'll call the spirit of discernment. Having engaged a vigorous washing or purging process, it would be easy to be less attentive at this stage of our endeavor. Yet, be mindful that a lax approach at this critical stage will produce experiences in your life that you are bound to find distasteful. They will prove synonymous with pouring water into a glass that has been poorly rinsed, and experiencing the undesirable flavor that soap residue has added to the water. So, be mindful to not simply splash a little water about and feel content that the task is complete. Listen to your Inner Guidance.

At this point, we've made contact with this guidance at many levels. It spoke through your soul as the voice of discontent - the instigator for your journey inward. It was your Spirit, posing the question: "Who Am I?" that prompted you to plow beneath the ultimately nonessential layers of false identity to unearth your true essence. Upholding its promise to "never leave nor forsake you," it has gone before you along every step of the path. Into each dark cavern of self-disclosure, each ominous cave of fear and doubt, it has cast its light of divine revelation, exhorting you to "Prepare the way of the Lord and make His paths straight." As the flowing waters of a perpetual waterfall having its origin at the throne of God, it is always available for us. Thus, this process of "conscious meditation" is about maintaining an open channel for spiritual guidance to flow through your affairs, at all times.

Having arrived at the point of embracing our true nature, we are clear about our unlimited opportunity to stand under its majestic stream. Its only request is that we take time to understand its majestic nature. As householder, landlord and patriarch of the Kingdom, though soft-spoken, Its rule is firm and irrevocable. It is the father figure in the story of the prodigal son who - when confronted with his son's desire for division and separation - acquiesced, knowing "that which comes from the Father is never separate, and that which goes out from the Father must return home again."

## A "Walking Meditation"

After having rinsed away the residual perceptions of false identity, separation, and altered-ego guidance, rendering our ego subject to the "higher power" provides a clean slate, as it denotes a willingness to release the past and have the Lord of the Kingdom delicately inscribe its inspiration upon the chalkboard of our Souls. As we remain open to spiritual guidance, we become an open conduit for spiritual illumination. As a result, each day of our life becomes a "walking meditation." All that is required is to make certain that we remain available, through continuing to walk in the light. Don't allow the requirements of day-to-day life to deafen your ear and draw you back into the illusory realm of societal interpretation. Take time to inquire whether there is guidance or inspiration available for whatever task you may be engaged in at the time. This could involve a matter as simple as what clothing to select for the day, what route to take to work or a general appeal for ideas about a particular area of focus.

Quite often, impacting relationships develop as a result of someone's attention having been drawn to what we are wearing. After having decided upon a last minute change of suit, shirt, blouse, skirt, jacket, or dress, we garner the attention of someone who voices an appreciation for our taste in clothing. Their comment leads to the discovery of common interests that foster further engagement. It could be that a decision to follow a nudge to take a different route to a familiar destination results in a significant "chance encounter." These and other experiences are examples of how our willingness to be more open and spontaneous, through listening to our intuitive cues, invests our lives with broader levels of experience and opportunity. So, make commitments to chase away fear and its limitations, and to become open and receptive to change. Be willing to follow an urge to do something different, to afford your life a chance to come alive with brand new possibilities.

As you consciously rinse away that which has been dredged-up for final elimination, allow the waters to flow liberally, so that all residue is rinsed away. Keep your eyes engaged. Inspect your work. Live consciously! Run your fingers across each surface of your life to caress its intricate details. If you find that you need to engage the washing process again, back up and do so. Refuse to compromise! Honor the intricate and wonderful process that your life truly is by allowing the incessant flow of the waters of life to bathe your soul. As the final remnants of illusion, discontent and resistance to your path of destiny are rinsed away, be mindful that you are preparing a vessel into which Divine Intent and Purpose are being poured.

## *Summary*

- That which comes from the Father (the Source) is never separate and must return again to its origin.

- Through allowing our lives to become a "walking meditation," we remain open to spontaneous spiritual guidance and the experience of synchronicity.

- This guidance is available for every issue we face in every aspect of our lives.

- Become willing to do things that are totally different from your established norms. This signals your openness to Spirit as well as your willingness to emerge from the box of habit and convention to explore the realm of spontaneous creativity.

A Task: List those things that you have routinely done one way that you can consciously decide to do in a totally different manner? Try them! This exercise sends the signal to your spiritual guidance that you are open to spontaneous creativity, along with unique perspectives that sponsor unlimited opportunities.

Affirmation: "In every moment of my life, I am aware of the presence of spiritual guidance in my affairs. As I engage the process of conscious meditation, I am forever bathing beneath the waterfalls of divine inspiration."

## Chapter 16

*Drying Your Dishes: The Process of Reflection*

"Blessed are the pure in heart: for they shall see God."
                                                    - Matthew 5:8

After all of your dishes are washed, rinsed and inspected, it's time to consider how you'll dry them. Basically, there are two drying methods: the more immediate hands-on approach of "towel drying" and the more ethereal, airy, laid-back approach of allowing them to "air dry." This analogy reminds me of television commercials that advertise dish washing detergents for both hand-washing and use in automatic dishwashers. The two most preeminent qualities touted are the absence of spots and/or film and the ability to see ones' clear reflection in the dish after it's washed. Having done a thorough job of washing and rinsing away all of the blockages, illusions and impediments of your "false self," rest assured that either the towel drying or air drying method will avail you a vessel without spot or blemish.

As a child, sitting alone in the woods, pondering my life and asking the "big questions," little did I know that I was perched at the very center of my destiny. Yet, this childhood bent toward solitude, introspection and reflection (the air drying method) availed me a realm of knowledge and understanding that is as universally accessible and free-flowing to each of us as the air we breathe. Following my urge to be in the woods placed me in an environment natural for openness and receptivity to the perpetual flow of inner communication. As I grew older and, like most, began to fill my life with outer activity, I was drawn away from this penchant for going within. As a result, my receptivity deafened to a certain extent, and my sensitivity to the "unseen realms" became obstructed. This led to a crisis in confidence that created an opening for an over-reliance on input from external sources. Yet, in embarking the journey back to self-awareness, I committed to return home to the center of my being, where I would sit in counsel with my inner knowing.

My approach to retuning myself to my "Self," incorporated a dual process of "outer-questing" or in-depth research (utilizing various books and cassette programs) coupled with other less mentally deliberate practices, such as meditation and simply sitting still and being quiet. While it remained important that I take in information provided by others, what was most important was that I go within, to see what their insights spoke to me, as an individual.

Along with spending substantial amounts of time in libraries and money in bookstores, I also gained tremendous insight and inspiration while walking, jogging and doing routine tasks. Among those tasks was washing dishes, an exercise to which I reverted often while writing this book. Other keys to restoring my sensitivity were found in choosing to "loosen-up" or to take myself less seriously, as well as in choosing to create more fun in my life. All in all, I discovered that the key to inviting powerful insights and keen self-analysis to become prominent occurrences (if not permanent fixtures in your daily life) is to remain present and receptive at all times is.

*Returning Home*

Prominent among my gifts is the ability to encourage and uplift, through sharing the insights gained from walking my unique path. And I marvel at the profoundness of having returned to the very point where I began, over sixty years ago. This ability to "return home" to ones' best self (to finally see oneself and others more clearly) is the principle objective of the drying process. Absent the costumes, makeup and role playing of the "Earth Theater Community," a truer image of you has gained clearance and can now emerge. It is at this stage that the profound truth of your natural gifts and talents (those things you have come qualified to share with the rest of humanity) are revealed. From the unfettered space of a pure heart into the reflective mirror of an enlightened consciousness comes the clear image of the "Master Self" - the prototypical man/woman, made in the image and likeness of the Creator. It is from this point of reflection that you can say with confidence, as did Jesus: (St. John 14:9) "He that hath seen me hath seen the Father."

## The Process of Reflection

Some of you will come to see that you are appointed "Divine Ushers." As such, you pave the way for unity through instigating a level of consciousness that spurs the elimination of hatred and discord among peoples. Uninhibited by racial prejudice, and endowed with the ability to see the larger truth in any situation, your gift is to share your innate understanding of the common thread that runs throughout the varied and seemingly fragmented concepts that encompass all religion, philosophy and spirituality. With your unique ability to bring people together, through an innate understanding of the common plight we share, you most directly reflect the spirit of human oneness. You understand that beneath our national, cultural, ethnic, and religious orientations, we are of one Source. You may find fulfillment working in areas that utilize your innate knowledge of how to incorporate the diverse aspects of various cultures into a harmonious whole. Your insight is key to aiding our efforts to do so, while continuing to honor our unique contribution to the human mosaic.

Others will have it revealed that yours is the gift of teaching others to accept love. Your genius can be utilized through encouraging individuals to love themselves and to accept nurturing from within and without. With your well-developed sense of humor and genuine love for humanity, you lighten the loads of those who feel weighted down and disheartened due to the weightiness of life circumstance. Through modeling self-love and teaching that only through loving ourselves can we truly love others, you help others to reclaim their power and to ascend above a victim's perspective. Clear that seeing oneself as a victim affords the one, sure, lifetime pass for a ride on the "merry-go-round of mediocrity," you promote the concept of self-love as the fuel necessary for rising above any circumstance. In promoting the love of self, in that the ability to love others is directly related to the ability to truly love oneself, you also facilitate the releasing of hatred and discord from the planetary consciousness. You may find that the greatest avenue for expression of your gift and for personal fulfillment is in areas that emphasize communication and various forms of artistic expression.

Some of you will discover that your mastery lies in teaching us to develop and maintain the strength of our own convictions. Your encouragement is to believe in ourselves, and to forge ahead in pursuit of the fulfillment of our dreams. The examples you set, through your self-motivated, persevering nature, inspire others to do that which is before them, and to not feel deprived by others. You also teach us to not become jealous or dependent upon others to pave the way for our success. Your gift may find its greatest expression on the path of the entrepreneur, leader or inventor. Your unique abilities to make your own way and not concern yourself with comparing your process to others facilitates the release of an unhealthy sense of competition from the planet.

To others, masterful insight is given concerning how we might establish more balance and harmony in our personal lives and in our interactions with others. You have come to teach balance and the "give and take" in all manner of relationship. You show us how to unearth those intricacies of human interaction that will enable us to establish "win/win situations" for all parties concerned. With your help, humanity can complete its move away from the type of interaction that seeks to win at the expense of another. Through the conscious release of your energy into the universe, the global energy of "us versus them" will begin to dissipate and dissolve into nothingness. This will pave the way for unprecedented, unilateral cooperation among people of all nations, religions, color, gender, and creeds. Yours is the gift of establishing mutually rewarding partnerships and cooperative business enterprises among those who may have previously considered themselves adversaries. This new business dynamic is a very important component to the new millennium mindset.

Still, others of you have come to the Earth as natural healers. Yours is the ability to help us to release our emotional blockages, and learn to deal with our emotional challenges in ways that build our souls. The opportunity to experience emotion and to utilize this critical resource in the creation and manifestation process lies at the root of our descent into the earth realm. In orer to protect our emotional nature from experiencing impulses that we consider to be harmful, we have developed a psuedo self-protection modality that has resulted in blockages in our emotional expression. Through your natural healing essence, you draw to your path those persons who are prone to "shutting off their feelings" and living in the external world. Being in your presence helps these persons to deal more openly with their feelings and to, thereby, dissolve and release the negativity of pent-up emotional distress. You teach us that we have the ability to heal ourselves and one another, by balancing and aligning the energies that pulsate through the various layers of our being.

In doing so, you elevate human consciousness to a new level of understanding in such areas as stress and health management.

These are but a few of the possibilities. Each unique and wonderful contribution we make lends to the overall enhancement of life on this planet, and the evolution of humanity. The key is to unlock the code that contains the intricate details of your unique contribution. You may choose to do so by following a prompting toward formal education so that you might "study to show yourself approved," allow your innate mastery to unfold at the behest of your inner guidance or both. Whatever route you choose, your particular area of mastery is certain to emerge when, from a pure heart, you gaze into the mirror of self-reflection. Your determination will be rewarded when you are willing to see yourself as a unique part of a unified endeavor to heal the earth and its inhabitants as we, ourselves, are healed.

*"The seed of God is in us. Pear seeds grow into pear trees, hazel seeds into hazel trees, and God seeds into God."*

-Meister Eckhart

## *Summary*

- The drying (reflection) process induces the ability to see your self and others more clearly.
- This process may unfold intellectually and/or intuitively, but must ultimately seat itself within your heart.
- In seeing yourself more clearly, you will see that you have been spiritually endowed with inherent gifts, talents, and abilities that await your discovery and implementation.
- These gifts are key to enhancing your life, and for uplifting humanity.
- Once the final residue of false identity has been rinsed away, you will come to see that you and the Father/ Mother principle (the Source of all things) and all of humanity are one.

A Task: Look back to your earlier years and consider what you sought to become as a child. In what carefree activity did you engage and imagine yourself gainfully employed? What is it that you would do with the bulk of your time if you could choose to do so this moment? What is it that stops you from doing so?

Affirmation: From out of my pure heart come praises, as I gaze into the mirror of my reflective consciousness and behold the image of the Creator.

# Chapter 17

## Staying Connected

*"God loves the world through us."*

—Mother Teresa

Quite often, the distance between our present reality and the reality we desire to experience is but a short leap in emotional awareness. This awareness endows us with the ability to discipline our responses to events and circumstances that emerge at critical points in our lives. To borrow a line from an R&B song popular in my youth, "It's a Thin Line Between Love and Hate." I use this line to underscore a common tendency that plagues us, as human beings. That tendency is to spend a great deal of time and emotional energy either straddling that line or attempting to walk its razor-sharp edge. Having one foot firmly planted in each dimension, we're resigned to "plucking pedals off of daisies," in a mindless game of "I love it/I love it not."

Holding our creative resources hostage within the dungeons of doubt and indecision, this double-minded approach of "non-committed commitment" and "disconnected connectedness" is the principal agent responsible for our inability to master our life circumstances and manifest our heart's true desire. It is also "the fly in the ointment" that spoils our attempts at creating mutually empowering relationships. To recall the term my mother used to voice her displeasure with some of my floor mopping efforts: "Half-assing" just won't get it done. Piquing the interest of our "Inner Genius" and enrolling it as our guide to the highly coveted prize of Life-Mastery takes passion, determination and a full-out commitment to doing all things well. Anything less and we're decidedly on our own.

### Indifference versus Detachment

While contemplating the essence of our struggle, it came to me that, collectively, our primary challenge rests with an inability to discern the difference between the dispositions of "detachment" and "indifference." Here is my take. If our desire is to be "spirit guided" or to have our life processes flow from within to without, the objective of detachment is a worthy one. Its aim is to endow us with discernment so that we understanding when to "pass the baton" to creative forces over which we have no conscious control. Having done a passionate job with all we know to do to advance our goals, detachment enables us to release all to that part of ourselves that is the "Amalgamator," or the one who knows how to bring all the various parts together to accomplish the end result.

Quite often, we only arrive at this point of surrender when we have wrestled and struggled with an issue, and become frustrated with our ability to manifest the desired result. In determining whether this or something better satisfies the need of our souls, it becomes the job of this "Spiritual Bonding Agent" to assess the motives and integrity that lie beneath our desires. It also bears the task of assigning value to the levels of passion and commitment we have generated around the tasks we've undertaken. These valuations are always in alignment with how you truly see yourself. Thus your advancement and the direction it takes are always on point. When our level of integrity or integration is such that we trust that we will draw to us the best and highest outcome that matches our vibration, our task is to surrender the process. And when our level of passion and demonstrated commitment to excellence match what is required to manifest our heart's desire, the Amalgamator gathers these energies and utilizes them to scour heaven and earth for the best connections and the most productive avenues for unfolding our desires.

When to be spiritually guided is only an after-thought, our altered egos will compel us to attach ourselves to certain outcomes and to hold out for them - at all costs. We will rigidly insist that our "truth" or soul validation can only unfold one way, or that our good can only come through one avenue. Ultimately, we discover that by maintaining this rigidity, we lock ourselves into a seat on the roller-coaster of misappropriated effort and regret. This experience creates an opening for the energy of indifference to creep into our affairs. Frequently born of a sense of failure, disappointment or being let down by significant others, the mindset of indifference is the ultimate breeding environment for mediocrity, lukewarmness and failure. Consequently, it is a mental state that should be avoided at all costs. In that it sucks and drains the creative vitality from our hearts and minds of all who stumble and fall into its tomb, its energy is most proficient at producing disconnected spiritual zombies. This often subtle and cleverly disguised energy renders us incapable of enthusiastically engaging new beginnings. It also renders us incapable of finishing what we began or bringing closure to past experiencs. It is also the energy behind our habits of not following-up with one another, as well resisting the simple act of making and maintaining eye contact. Emitting a vibe which says "I don't know you, so your plight doesn't matter to me," a life plagued with the energy of indifference clearly signals a loss of integrity or integration with the spiritual part of one's being.

While the energy of indifference says: "I don't care," a posture of "detachment says "While I care quite deeply, I am aware of the need to allow and maintain a level of causal trust between us." This posture creates the space for others to pursue that which works for their highest good, in accord with the good of all others. Therefore, detachment says, "I release, let go, and allow the Spirit to engage and do its work in you as well as me." While Indifference says "I'm not enrolled, so I don't have a desire or preference," detachment says "I am clear about my desires, though committed to not generate an emotional storm if those desires are not met."

A commitment to grasp and employ a proper understanding of these two energies will enable us to release others to work their lives as they see fit. It will empower us to release a tendency for resentfully withdrawing from their lives when they make it clear that we are imposing. Your quest for Life-Mastery and Spiritual Genius will be well served by your diligent effort to draw a clear distinction between these energies, so that you will clearly know when one or the other is working in your life. This clarity will empower you to make needed adjustments that may prevent you from crossing the line between love and hate.

After trying and so often failing to reach our goals, fearing future failure, it's not uncommon that we adjust our sights to levels that our wounded sense of accomplishment presents as more attainable. In the event things don't work out according to Plan A, in order to not lose faith, we build in contingencies and "B Plans." While some of this appears to be sound business strategy, the potential trap lies in not realizing that a basic requirement for fulfilling your dreams is that you have dreams that you are clear and committed to as well as passionate about. When that is so, your spirit will provide enough kindlin' to keep the fire burning. Sometimes while all obstructions are burned away and the path is being cleared, that flame may wane to a flicker or pilot light status. But, fear not! Your level of connectedness and commitment will enable you to remain passionate, regardless of inner challenges or outward appearances.

Once you have recovered the vision of who you are born to be, despite how far you may feel you have fallen, commit to raising the bar. Start again with renewed vitality. Having comprehended and integrated the essentials of this dishwashing or "soul purging" process, you should be clear that you have the power to bounce back the first, second, third, fourth, or hundredth time you experience disheartening challenges. Trust that there are no insurmountable reverses. It's not only reasonable, but highly likely that you may not see, with absolute clarity, the total blueprint of your dream. You may have only glimpsed an image that may require many adjustments before it is properly and powerfully focused and integrated into your conscious awareness. Unless you already have the material means for bringing your vision and plans to fruition, you will be required to trust that the method by which they will manifest exists somewhere beyond your comprehension. Yet, the facts remain that you must have dreams and desires that you are passionate about, and that you must not allow the energy of indifference to get anywhere near those dreams. As an added though crucial admonishment, once discovered, you must conquer your fear, and move confidently toward your destiny.

*"If the world is gonna be a better place, it all depends on the human race; the future rests on things we hold inside. A heart darkened with fear and hate can never truly intimidate enlightened hearts that cast all fear aside."*

- It's A "God Thang" - Raja

Not all dreams concern the pursuit of material wealth, social status, fame, political power, or success in such tangible terms. In fact, to place ones' focus on these things as an exclusive or ultimate objective would signal an attachment to living in the soon to be excavated public housing project of "old paradigm thinking." The objective of this book, and particularly this chapter, is to encourage you to get in touch and stay connected with a "larger purpose" for your life - to utilize it as motivation for the goals you set and the roles you choose to play. Bear in mind that the materialization of the dream of discovering your inner light and helping to create a new world requires the same level of passion and commitment as any other objective. It also requires money and other resources. The key remains a willingness to passionately connect with your vision and stay fired up - despite any and all challenges, false starts, set-backs, and obstacles. In short, the clarity of your vision must be unmistakable, and your commitment to seeing it actualized must be unshakable.

## A Willingness to Persevere

There are many real-life accounts of visionaries whose passion for the attainment of an ideal greater than themselves was felt deeply and burned brightly. History shares how they endured punishment and ridicule, while overcoming seemingly insurmountable odds and obstacles to bringing their visions to fruition. Men such as Martin Luther King Jr., Nelson Mandela and Thomas Edison typify a mastery level of dedication, patience and perseverance. Dr. King had a dream of equality for all people, with no regard for race or socio/economic status. His example of "Kingdom Work" was pivotal for reversing the tide of legalized segregation and hatred in these United States and abroad. Through a willingness to rise above reticence and fear, he spurred a movement of nonviolent protest that has proved to be a continuous and potent initiator of positive change. Though his dedication ultimately cost him his life, even in death he remains a powerful instrument for moving us toward a deeper search for our commonality and humanity. His is a grand testament to a "greater love" that would cause a man to lay down his life for his friends.

Nelson Mandela's story is one of the greatest accounts of dedication and perseverance of our time. His commitment to an apartheid-free South Africa landed him in prison for a period of twenty-seven years. To emerge from these suppressive and debilitating circumstances to become President of South Africa is a an accomplishment that borders on folklore. This demonstration of his willingness to persevere is the epitome of a commitment to serve your calling despite the cost. To do so is the epitome of life mastery. To do so without bitterness is Godly. His demonstration speaks volumes about the level of commitment, patience, perseverance, and true freedom he developed prior to his imprisonment. How he emerged from captivity reflects how he maintained his integrity while facing a seemingly irreversible challenge to his vision of freedom for all the people of South Africa. It also provides clear evidence of the benefits inherent in holding true to ones' vision.

Edison's pursuit of the electric light motivated him to press through well over five-thousand failed experiments before arriving at his point of success. Time after time he failed, yet he never once resigned himself to failure. Ultimately, he accomplished what he went after, and the whole world has benefited from his unrelenting nature. There are other sterling examples of those who - at the behest of their Godhood - embraced a vision that transcended personal gain. George Washington Carver used his Genius to extract unlimited possibilities from what appeared to be limited or useless commodities. Though born a slave, as an agricultural chemist at Tuskegee Institute, he dedicated his life to bettering the plight of African Americans, by discovering ways to generate new economic possibilities. Where perseverance is concerned, he is quoted as having said "Pray as though everything depended upon God, and work as though everything depends upon you." Having discovered hundreds of uses for the peanut, sweet potato and soybean, and devised many products from cotton waste, his contributions were of paramount importance to improving the economy of the post Civil War South.

Who can overlook the spirit of the incomparable Mother Teresa? Her mission and passion centered around a desire to bring comfort, love and a sense of human dignity to those who suffered the ravages of terminal illness, abject poverty and war. From the age of seventeen until the day she made her transition, her heart went out to perpetually comfort those who mourned. Yet, she understood that the attainment of her mission required the practical application of worldly business principles. This understanding kept her on top of, and in touch with the financial side of her worldwide outreach.

Then there is Yeshua ben Joseph, whom we commonly know as Jesus. His revealing example of our indelible connection with the Father opened a way for us to remember our heritage and remain connected to our Source. Biblical history has recounted but few of the wonderfully miraculous deeds of his public ministry. What we do know is that he infused each act he engaged with the spirit of passion and connectedness. There is a story of his entering the temple at Jerusalem, overturning the tables of the money changers, and chasing them out. After having, on several occasions, commanded them to leave, he confronted them with whip in hand, and a passionate determination to remove them from the temple, and he did so. With this same resolve, we must overturn the tables of our emotional lukewarmness, and with passion and perseverance, turn the table on those patterns of divided thought and feeling that set up shop in our temple. These are the energies that seduce us into exchanging our connection with spiritual guidance for a attitude of resignation and indifference. By rendering us dispassionate and apathetic, indifference - when confused with and substituted for detachment - can dilute or even diffuse the higher frequencies of the creative energy of our souls. When this occurs, the best we can do is sell out, or muddle around in a state of mediocrity, when our true calling is to Life Mastery.

## *Summary*

- Our best efforts are often undermined by our tendency to vacillate between two levels of commitment, as well as two opinions, about our ultimate success.

- An understanding of the difference between the energies of detachment and indifference is crucial to remaining passionate, despite the appearance of a lack of progress.

- Come what may, in spite of any obstacles or setbacks, the passion that you generate around your ideas and dreams will empower you to persevere.

## The Tao of Dishwashing

A Task: Take a moment to list areas where you have allowed yourself to become indifferent, disconnected and unconcerned. What adjustments can you make to better align yourself with an appropriate sense of the energy of detachment?

Affirmation: "As I move to align my emotional energies for optimum performance, I release any tendency toward indifference, and allow a healthy sense of detachment to find its rightful place in my nature."

# Chapter 18

## *Where is Your Talent?*

*"Thou hath been faithful over a few things, I will make thee ruler over many things."*
-Matthew 25:21

### *Your Soul as the Ultimate Dish*

Dishes, in this story, are a metaphor for several things. They represent the many ways our soul lends itself in service - i.e., the roles we play as parent, spouse, lover, student, counselor, employee, employer, minister, and friend. They are also my way of referring to the issues with which we grapple, as we interrelate with others in these variable roles. The ultimate aim of "The Tao of Dishwashing" is to bring you to the realization that, in truth, there is but one dish - the Collective Human Soul. The nature of that soul is that of a repository for the various energies that contribute to shaping our humanity, or making us who we are. In preparing our souls for the new millennium, our task is to retrieve, align and distill the various and, seemingly, multifarious aspects of ourselves into a concentric whole. It is at this point of wholeness - the point of merging all the individual pieces of serviceware into one utilitarian vessel - that Mastery makes its presence known in the earth. It is then that the reward for our aggregate effort will manifest and foster benefits that will acknowledge our individuality in ways that exceed our wildest expectations.

To remain vital and viable in the midst of the coming changes, it's wise to contemplate how to posture yourself for service. Consider that, for you, it is an unquestionable expectation that the cup that holds your tea or coffee, or the glass from which you drink water, juice or wine, and the plate upon which your meal is piled are clean. It is also a given that we expect them to be served from skillets, pots, pans, bowls, platters, pitchers, and carafes that are also clean. The same is so with your soul - the vessel from which you offer your service to the world. Just as you would, most likely, not knowingly drink from a dirty glass, the same is so for those souls with whom you interact. Despite how accepting they appear, they too have no appreciation for being offered no choice but to drink lukewarm water from an unclean vessel - a vessel covered with the film of dishonesty, self-hatred, racial prejudice, religious arrogance, or sexism.

Though prompted by hardship, as we move through the new millennium, the rapid rate at which we avail ourselves to new information and experiences (from within and without) will provide unparalleled opportunity to create and embrace constructive change. We can begin to prepare now, by deciding to live consciously, through embracing our divine right to define who we are and how we interact with others. We also have the choice to continue burying our heads in the sand. Be clear, though, that there are costs associated with failing to face ourselves in the mirror of our innermost intent. Those costs manifest as experiences born of the results of your creative subconscious creeping up on you...unawares.

In the way of conscious preparation, I encourage you to examine the source of your inspiration to discover what kindles a fire inside of you and causes you to bring forth your best from the core of your being. What is it that touches the inherently humanitarian nature within your soul, sparks its angelic essence and calls it forth? In your pursuit of Life-Mastery and personal fulfillment, it would serve you well to find a way to live out of this "core energy" at all times. Commit to transferring it to every endeavor to which you lend your creative energy. This includes all of your interactions with people, places and things - familiar and unfamiliar...seen and unseen.

## The "Little Foxes" that Destroy the Vine

Quite often, for many, the task of dishwashing does not include a consideration for restoring the washing environment to order. This became quite evident while monitoring my teenage daughter's dishwashing efforts. For her, there seemed to be no connection between washing the dishes and, say, properly draining the sink and wiping off the counters. Yet, once the dishwashing is complete, it is just as important to do the "supplemental things" that are, seemingly, incidental to the task. Taking care of any "loose ends" is essential to preventing the unraveling of the work you have so diligently knitted together. You must drain and clean the sink - including the faucets, return the detergent and other tools to their respective places and wipe-off the counter and surrounding areas. These areas include stove tops, microwaves and table tops. Once complete, rinse out the dish rag and put it and the dish towel in an orderly place. The same level of commitment to the overall objective is true as it relates to the Tasking a Master Soul, or the process of purging and invigorating your soul essence.

There is a Buddhist proverb which says: "Before enlightenment, chop wood, carry water; after enlightenment, chop wood, carry water." I share it as a reminder that the fundamental things that brought you to this point of "self-actualization" are required to help you stay the course. So, while I encourage you to not needlessly "sweat the small stuff," in one sense, be mindful that, as is stated in Songs of Solomon 2:15 (in the King James version of the bible): "it is the little foxes that destroy the vine." If you can fine-tune and intensify your inner vision and use it to scope out and eliminate the nuances implied by this bit of wisdom, you will unleash a tremendous power to master your life and advance your affairs.

To remain receptive to the growth-inducing information available from your own Spirit, I recommend that you become diligent about pulling aside to be still to listen to your heart. As you evolve to the space of honoring yourself as the "true church," you may discover value in being as uncomplicated, inconspicuous and spontaneous as possible in your practice. Yet, if you have a special place (in your physical environment) where you go to pull aside, honor this time and intent as sacred. In doing so, when you enter into it, you elevate your mind to a higher level of expectancy and are apt to receive greater benefits. Make this space as clutter-free as possible. This sends your mind the signal that, upon entering, you agree to leave the extraneous concerns of the outer world behind. Whatever it takes, be firm in your commitment to a practice of self-sustained spiritual nurturing, and to the development of inner peace.

If you are benefiting from an association with religious institutions or other forms of collective worship, honor these alliances by contributing your support in helping maintain their viability. Whether your contribution is money, volunteer time or any other assistance with holding and manifesting a collective vision, the principle of giving and receiving will respond to your commitment to being not only considerate, but generous with your resources. Also, never consider any task too minor and mundane or your talent too great or too small and insignificant to give your best effort. Your potential for stewardship over greater opportunity and resources is built upon the foundation you establish with the opportunities you have now.

## *The Parable of the Talents*

There is a parable found in the 25th chapter of the Book of Matthew (King James version) beginning at verse 14, which reads as follows: "For the kingdom of heaven is as a man traveling into a far country, who called his own servants and delivered unto them his goods. And unto one he gave five talents, to another, two, and to another one; to every man according to his several ability; and straightway took his journey. Then he that had received the five talents went and traded with the same, and made them other five talents. And likewise he that had received two, he also gained other two. But he who had received one went and digged in the earth and hid his lord's money.

After a long time the lord of those servants cometh, and reckoneth with them. And so he that had received five talents came and brought other five talents, saying, Lord, thou deliverest unto me five talents: behold, I have gained beside them five talents more. His lord said unto him, Well done, thou good and faithful servant, thou has been faithful over a few things, I will make thee ruler over many things: enter thee into the joy of thy lord. He also that had received two talents came and said, Lord, thou deliverest unto me two talents: behold I have gained two other talents beside them. His lord said unto him, Well done, good and faithful servant; thou has been faithful over a few things, I will make thee ruler over many things: enter thou into the joy of thy lord.

Then he which had received the one talent came and said; Lord, I knew thee that thou art an hard man, reaping where thou has not sown, and gathering where thou hast not strawed: And I was afraid, and went and hid the talent in the earth: lo, there, thou hast that which is thine. His lord answered and said unto him, Thou wicked and slothful servant, thou knewest that I reap where I sowed not, and gather where I have not strawed: Thou oughtest therefore to have put my money to the exchangers, and then at my coming I should have received mine own with usury. Take therefore the talent from him, and give it unto him which hath ten talents. For unto every one that hath shall be given, and he shall have abundance: but from him that hath not shall be taken away even that which he hath."

# Where is Your Talent?

What have you done with your talent? Remember, we all have destinys, callings and life purposes, as well as the gifts, talents and abilities to bring these commitments to fruition. If you have yet to discover yours, the roots can often be found in our childhood fantasies, dreams and aspirations. It seems that we were more connected to our unlimited nature then. Somewhere along the way, we allowed what others had to say about our lives and life in general to mesmerize, hypnotize and seduce us into burying our talents and surrendering our dreams in favor of the false illusion of worldly security. Such ideas as "Life is hard, unrelenting and unfair," and "You have to get serious and work hard to create stability and security" were handed down to us with good intent, by our parents, teachers and other "success trainers." Though this is obviously the picture they had of life as well as the truth they chose to build their lives upon, the predominant yearning within the collective soul of humanity is forever moving toward creating and living out of a more liberating, fulfilling, dynamic, and wholesome reality.

## *Polo Horses*

A story from Taoism tells of a carefree band of horses that galloped spiritedly around the hills and meadows. They dined on green grass and drank clear water from cool streams. Living freely and naturally, they lived contentedly. Along came a famous horse-trainer named Polo. He captured the unsuspecting horses, declaring, "I know what is best for them." He bridled the horses, decorated them with cheap ornaments and gave them numbers. Then he made them perform in public. They were forced to trot about in precise formation to the cracking commands of a whip. The once carefree horses turned into mechanical performers - tired, sick, afraid.

This story strikes a familiar parallel to the lives many lead today - lives that look inviting and seem to be in precise formation. Yet, when the truth is had, they are, at best, shallow, dis-empowering and without lasting reward. Having allowed ourselves to be "rounded-up" and herded into busy little, tailor-made, picturesque existence's, we've become trapped in an arena where, with no regard for inner contentment, the emphasis is on appearance and public performance. After having settled for the cheap, decorative, designer lifestyles synonymous with Polo Horses, we are left to work through our inner chaos in quiet desperation - saddled beneath the weight of dead-end jobs, out-moded relationships, and dis-empowering belief systems. It seems that some are quite comfortable and content with their Polo imprint, and may even consider it a sign that their talent or Genius is firmly in hand. These so called "status symbols" may even grant a sense of certainty that your feet are firmly planted on the path of your divine destiny, and this may indeed be so. But be careful not to delude yourself. Be mindful that in choosing to not surrender to the guidance of intuitive wisdom, the satisfaction derived from exercising your talents (no matter how extraordinary) will be limited to worldly accomplishment and acclaim. Bear in mind that it's not uncommon to look the part of a Master Soul while your inner being withers and melts away under the sweltering spotlight of unrealized Genius. While you may consider yourself "king of the world" where the trappings of worldly accomplishment are concerned, this outward approach to inner satisfaction will ultimately foster creative impotence, inner chaos and utter disappointment. When it is all said and done, you may find yourself confronting this adaptation of the notable biblical question: "What does it profit me to gain the whole world and lose out on aligning with soul's intent?"

At points along our journey to wholeness, in that it is the Father's good pleasure to give us the kingdom, it is our opportunity to experience all that life has to offer - to have each and every one of our desires met. The ultimate opportunity is to have those desires met while maintaining a sense of balance, wholeness and inner integrity. It is important for you to know that you are in total ownership of your creative energies, and that you bear the responsibility for moving under your own power toward spiritually empowering goals and objectives. I encourage you to live with great passion and a deeply abiding commitment to humanity and to honor the humanity of others. To operate otherwise is the epitome of mediocrity and a sure path to the thwarting and imminent death of your creative energies. This is a dire price to pay in exchange for the fleeting moments of appreciation and admiration that come from those who exalt others because they have no true sense of their own inner light.

## A "Self-test"

As a test to determine if you are truly free or whether someone or something "has your number," you might ask yourself the following questions or a few of your own: In the context of your relationships, are there those who know just how to "pull your strings" and manipulate you into surrendering your desires to please them? Does the work you

## Where is Your Talent?

do (whether employed by self or others) place such a demand on your energy that it creates an imbalance where family, social, spiritual, and personal quality time issues are concerned? Is this assessment of imbalance something you can see, agree with and own, or is this someone else's assessment that flies counter to what your heart says is best and highest for all concerned? Are the highest times of your spiritual life those spent in church and, therefore, you can hardly wait for the doors to open so that you can "assemble with like minded souls" or "escape the ravages of this world." Is the minister of your church or your favorite televangelist so far into your business that to make a decision without their consultation and blessing would seem an affront against God?

When challenges enter your life to test your desire for spiritual growth and maturity, is your most common response to seek out an enemy (be it the devil or someone or something else) to blame rather than taking ownership, and embracing the occasion as an opportunity for personal growth? Finally: Does your view of the world unfold within the limited context of basic black or white, saint or sinner, right or wrong, them versus us, or mine versus yours, with an occasional allowance for shades of gray?

As we chart our spiritual course for the new millennium, a brief yet honest review of our lives to-date will reveal that, collectively, we have done ourselves a grave disservice by giving our power away through proclaiming ourselves victims. We are due to come face to face with the indelible results of limiting our perception of the sway we hold over our lives and deferring the responsibility for running our lives to the self-serving agendas of others. Failing to listen to our own hearts will render us drained of our creative inspiration and stripped of our willingness to trust our inherent ability for self-renewal. As a result, like the Polo horses, we will have become and will remain sick, tired, and afraid.

For untold sums of people, the effects have already proved deadly. Seeking a reprieve from the merry-go-round of myth, mayhem and misery, refuge is sought and found in a hypodermic needle, crack pipe, opioids, or more speedy forms of exodus and escape. No longer willing to embrace the illusion, with freedom as the ultimate objective, they seek and find liberation through the most expedient means available...including suicide.

## The Wonderful News

It doesn't take a great deal of imagination to picture the world as it would appear given twenty more years of traveling down our current path. The fact that an inordinate amount of our collective attention and resources remain focused on managing the effects of our fearful state rather than discovering and working to heal its cause, sets the stage for many more years of heightened unrest. Though it often appears that the average citizen has grown deeply numb in the face of the violence, hatred and general chaos that pervades our world, I can't imagine that the human spirit will continue to endure an assault that is mounting so quickly that it threatens to obliterate the essence of human nature. The wonderful news for this newly dawning age is that true and unbridled freedom is yet attainable. Ultimately, the soul's quest for freedom and reconciliation must be satisfied. You can choose freedom, in this very moment, by deciding to recover your talent, restore your soul and prepare it to make the transition into the higher realm of "Kingdom Service." Though it will most likely require some digging, the fact that you are still "alive and kicking" affords you the opportunity to engage the search. By unearthing the "key" (your invaluable creative gift and Genius) you will be able to utilize its tremendous potential for balancing and harmonizing your energy. When this synthesis occurs, it will usher bounty and increase into all areas of your life.

If, for years, you've remained stuck in the mire of self-deprecating behavior, your earnest desire to engage the path to your higher calling makes this your time. Regardless of how deeply stuck and frustrated you may have become, you can reverse your plight if you can find the fortitude to capture the inspiration of a single moment. Aligning with your true spiritual nature will place you in conscious charge of your dynamic and perpetually unfolding destiny. The only requirement is that you sincerely desire to emerge from your walking dream. To reclaim your birthright, you must pull off the old and put on the new. My experience of crying out from the wilderness is that, if you are sincere about making the connection to inner guidance, when you cry out, "Lord, Lord," the Master Dishwasher will say "Here am I." All that is required is that you become willing, ready and receptive to stepping into your calling.

Reconnecting with the energy of intuitive guidance will lead you to the spot where your talent lies buried, and assist you in recovering it. You may find that it shines and glistens like new money, or it may be covered with mud, and bear witness to years of neglect. It may even show signs of rust and disrepair; but don't despair. When you employ the faith to engage your talent for bringing wholeness to your life and the lives of others, your desire will draw to you others who will lend their talents to assist in manifesting your vision. There is bound to be among them someone who is masterful in aiding you with dusting off and restoring your talent to its original and inherent glory.

Mustering the courage to dig a little (to look beyond the veil of illusion) will allow you to, again, see with clear vision that which is and always was - your "Authentic Self" as the "Master Dishwasher" and owner of the restaurant, which is your individual domain within the collective Kingdom. This pride of ownership will gift you with a renewed responsibility for safeguarding the integrity of that which you offer others in service to their humanity. It is then that you will come to know yourself as the "Master Chef" of every meal that has shown up on your plate. You will then see, with great clarity, that you are the creator of all that your life is, was and ever will be. You will then becom empowered to serve others as a vessell worthy of honor. You have but to ask, and it shall be given. Seek and ye shall find.

*Making the Leap*

What will it take for you to surrender to the unlimited potential for Genius and Mastery that lies dormant within you? Do you love and trust yourself enough to move toward the grandest vision you can imagine for yourself? Is this your moment? Are you willing to seize it? Are you ready to make the leap or is the fear of what others will think of your moving from convention into unlimitedness holding you back? As you stand poised for transformation, as an additional boost, I share this quote from French novelist and critic, Georges Bataille (1897-1962):

> *"At man's core there is a voice that wants him never to give in to fear. But if it is true that, in general, man cannot give in to fear, at the very least he postpones, indefinitely, the moment when he will have to confront himself with the object of his fear...when he will no longer have the assistance of reason as guaranteed by God, or when he will no longer have the assistance of God such as reason guaranteed. It is necessary to recoil, but it is necessary to leap, and perhaps one only recoils in order to leap better."*

We can all agree that the world is changing. Our evolution into greater awareness of who we are as spiritual beings is compelling us to awaken. to This clarion call is an urge to quest for the higher calling of our Divine Selves. In working to define how we will shape the next thousand years of our soul's journey, your contribution - your unique talent and Genius - is needed. The essence of you is an important insert to the new mosaic that is being woven within collective consciousness. Hopefully, this book adds kindlin' to the fire beneath your commitment to being the most naturally unfolding, self-actualized, joyous person you can possibly be. That is the essence of your true Self. So, I encourage you to release yourself from the prisons of fear and criticism constructed by yourself and others, and embrace the path that will lead to the unleashing of your Genius into the world. Cast your bread upon the waters. Allow nothing to stop you from living the life you were born to live. This life of creativity and connectedness has only those boundaries and limitations that we impose upon our imagination and commitment to wholeness.

And last, but not least - lest I forget; as a final step to "Tasking a Master Soul," to remove any trace of doubt that you are anything other than a magnificent being, sweep the floor and take out the trash!

Raja

## *Summary*

- Dishes represent the many ways we lend ourselves in service, as well as the issues we wrestle with on our way toward Mastery.

- Our principle life objective is to align or merge the multiple aspects of self into one concentric whole.

- This "wholeness" is evident within the soul that has developed Mastery in life.

- Doing the supplemental things (remaining mindful of the details) keeps us aligned with the basic principles that are responsible for creating our success.

- It is an honorable thing to support those alliances and other sources that contribute to our growth.

- Establish a pact with yourself to secure a space and time to regularly turn aside and go within. Honor this time and space as sacred, by making it a priority, and by tending to it as such.

- Never consider a task too mundane or your talent too small or large to give your best effort. Your future opportunities for steward-ship are built upon how you tend to the responsibility you have accepted to date.

- We all have gifts and talents which, when properly understood and best utilized, lend to our life-purpose, destiny, and roles in shaping the world.

- Ideas - passed on by our parents, teachers and significant others - are often behind our decisions to bury our talents and surrender our dreams, in exchange for a sense of "security."

- The act of reviewing and/or revisiting your childhood dreams, fantasies, and desires could spark a remembrance of where your talents he buried.

- A simple "self-test" will help you to determine whether you are truly your own person, or whether someone or something else is "pulling your strings."

# The Tao of Dishwashing

- You can choose freedom by deciding to recover your talent, restore your soul and prepare it to make the transition into the higher realm of "Kingdom service."

Where is Your Talent?

They Said You Were Not Ready!
a poem by Raja

They said you were not ready
and wouldn't be for years
in spite of all your heartache  disillusionment and tears

They said you would not answer
though I came knocking at your door,
said you'd adjusted to the cancers
of injustice, crime and war

And even though I'd cry out
from a pure unfettered heart
they said you wouldn't have the will
to set yourself apart

They said it would take a catastrophe
like hostile visitors from space
to incite, arouse, and galvanize
the entire human race

Said your life's already ordered
and that you haven't "seen" enough
that you couldn't make a stand for change
that you really aren't that tough

Said to give you two or three more years
or maybe five to ten
You'd see the product of your fears
said, "You'd be ready then!"

Yes, I've seen you in my sleep at night
while traveling to and fro
I've teetered on the brink of fright
at just how far you'll go

To tempt and test the hand of fate
to thumb your nose at time
while breathing waning, bated breath

into a dying paradigm
And, yet I can't just sit and wait
until disaster calls
therefore you'll find me at the gate
and in your hallowed halls

I'll be the one to sound the bell
I may blow Gabriel's horn
I'll tug the guide-strings of your heart
I'll shout, arouse, forewarn

For as I live and shall not die
my hope within remains
To see the whole of humanity
united on the plains

So when you hear me knocking
though peaking through the blinds
release the captive of your hearts
and free your fettered minds

For I come not to do you harm
or that you'd worship me
I come to caste a piercing light
to set your spirit free

Though they said you were not ready
and wouldn't be for years,
will you cast your fate to the quibbling
of your falsehoods, doubts and fears?

## *Other Works and Services offered by Raja:*

- The Tao of Dishwashing - Tasking a Master Soul - Audio Book
- The Shift from Sheep to Shepherd of Your Own Soul - A Life Purpose Manifesto - Paperback and/or Audio Book
- The Art of Living - What Do I Think About It? - Dual Disc Musical Presentation
- Personal Life Path/Life Purpose Consultations

## *Upcoming:*

- A PhD in Being Me - A Path to Grounding, Growing and Gifing Your True Self
- The Elimination of Fear Paperback and Audio Book

## *Contact:*

email: rajaiam@yahoo.com and raja@rajaiam.com

website: rajaiam.com